LONDON BOROUGH OF ENFIELD
LIBRARY SERVICES

This book to be RETURNED on or before the latest date stamped
unless a renewal has been obtained by personal call, post or
~~telephone~~, quoting the above number and the date due for return.

THE ART OF DYING

THE ART OF DYING

IAN CRICHTON

PETER OWEN · LONDON

ISBN 0 7206 0353 6

PETER OWEN LIMITED

20 Holland Park Avenue London W11 3QU
First British Commonwealth edition 1976
© 1976 Ian Crichton

Printed in Great Britain by
Villiers Publications Ltd London

The art of living well and the art of dying well are one.

EPICURUS

CONTENTS

ACKNOWLEDGEMENTS

First, I must record my gratitude to Roger Musgrave and David Le Vay. To Roger Musgrave for suggesting and initiating this project, and for invaluable help given during the preparation of the book; to David Le Vay for his work on Chapters 4 and 5, concerning the medical aspects of death, and for his succinct account of his views on euthanasia.

I must also thank Michael Williams for guiding me through the maze of facts and figures concerning death; Dr Cicely Saunders at St Christopher's Hospice for sparing her valuable time and allowing me to study the important work that is being done there; Dr P. M. Sutton, Reader in Pathology at University College Hospital Medical School, London, for his expert advice; the principals of the funeral firms who generously allowed Roger Musgrave and myself to visit their premises and who answered our questions so frankly; and all those others, laymen and professionals, who co-operated with me during my research. My thanks, too, to Dan Franklin, my editor at Peter Owen.

The tables on pages 28 and 34 are reproduced with the permission of the Controller of Her Majesty's Stationery Office.

I.C.

1 | THE LAST TABOO

He that fears death lives not.
GEORGE HERBERT

'That's *morbid*!' is the usual response when people hear you are writing a book about death and dying. But this expression of disgust and fear, with its accompanying grimace, may be a good reason for the book's existence.

Reacting against the slaughter in two World Wars, the Victorian era's love of funeral pomp, and too much poetic romanticism ('I have been half in love with easeful death', wrote Keats), we tend to lean too far the other way.

Death is feared, postponed as long as possible, hidden from sight, 'swept under the carpet', and banned from polite conversation out of the kindest of motives. ('But I *wanted* to talk about him,' protested a widow complaining that all her friends and relatives had conspired to protect her from any mention of her husband, so that it had seemed as though he had never existed.)

Modern frankness and the demand for facts from an increasingly aware public have dissipated some of the mists cloaking the subject of death, yet it remains the final great unmentionable, the last taboo, and its mysteries are as awesome and tantalizing to us as those of sex were to our Victorian ancestors. The perennial popularity of horror films and the emergence of a new cult of 'screen violence' corroborate this proposition. Death, not sex, is now the taboo whose violation – *in fiction* – provides the ultimate titillation. *Le vice anglais,* that predilection for cruel and terrifying spectacles, can be indulged today as never before. But home from the cinema, back in reality, mention of death – one's own, or that of a friend or relative – is once again firmly prohibited.

11

Of course, this tendency to avoid looking death in the eye is not solely a failing of the British. In Australia, for instance, there are strict rules about transporting coffins anywhere in that continent: they must be placed in boxes or wrapped in heavy protective paper, and the outside must be marked with the sign of an empty champagne bottle – so that nobody will know that they are coffins. In America the funeral industry makes great endeavours to ensure that a corpse does not look as though it is dead. While gathering material for this book, I wrote to thirty-two foreign embassies and high commissions; of these only half replied. A measure of their indifference, perhaps, or was I violating a taboo?

This book, then, gives the facts. It attempts to lift the veils obscuring how and why people die, for knowledge often brings comfort and banishes fears and may make it easier for us to accept our inevitable end. The Tibetans, for example, are taught to face death not only calmly but clear-mindedly and heroically. The future of the living, according to them, depends on a proper death. They feel that so to die is an art, and one that is little known in the West. In contrast, they are puzzled by our unwillingness to die, and by our making every effort to interfere with the process of death. In Tibet, the Art of Dying is every bit as important as the Art of Living.

The book covers attitudes to death in Western, Eastern and primitive societies, and gives some statistical facts on death rates, causes of death, longevity and life expectancy. There are medical details about the point at which death occurs, what happens to the body after death, what happens when people donate their bodies to science, resuscitation, euthanasia and 'cryonics' (the extraordinary study and practice of the refrigeration of human bodies in the hope of their subsequent revival). There is a section on the complicated legal aspects of handling and disposing of bodies, inquests, death duties and wills, and another on the undertaking industry, embalming, crematoria and funerals both civil and military. A further section recounts the experiences of men and women who have 'died' yet survived, and those of people who have faced approaching death. Also represented are the views of some terminal patients, whose courage and cheerfulness were an inspiration to everyone around them – not least to the author of this book.

Talking to many doctors and nurses in the course of my research, and reading other works on the subject, I was relieved to find the same phrase cropping up again and again : 'In my experience, most people die peacefully, quietly, and often while they are unconscious'. A recent study showed that two-thirds of those who died in a hospital or institution were unconscious at the time. Sir William Osler, a physician who died in 1919, said that he had made careful records at the death-beds of 500 people : 'Ninety suffered bodily pain or distress of one sort or another, eleven showed mental apprehension, two positive terror, and one expressed spiritual exaltation, one bitter remorse'. But the great majority, he said, gave no sign one way or the other. 'Their death was a sleep and a forgetting.'

Personally, I fear a lengthy and distressing illness, or the tedious deteriorations of old age, far more than death. If we are unlucky and have to face suffering at the end of our days, death comes as a welcome relief. But at least we can hope for a more merciful departure, and from what I have seen can count ourselves lucky to live in a civilized society, where increasing attention is being paid to the problem of soothing terminal pain.

I do not know what comes after death, and hold no orthodox religious views. But I have come to believe that the death of my body will not mean the end of my being. Like so many of the world's millions, of many different faiths, I find this comforting.

2 | ATTITUDES TO DEATH

> Death is a camel that lies down
> at every door.
> PERSIAN PROVERB

The ways in which men have looked upon death have, over the centuries, combined dread with sympathy for the bereaved and a highly practical attitude towards the dead spirit. Either the spirit had to be propitiated for fear of the harm it might do to the living, which meant flattering it with food or elaborate rituals, or it could be used as a focal point for the prayers which gave solace to the bereaved, or it could be sent on its perilous journey with loving wishes for its safety.

Death has been portrayed by a wide variety of symbols, including straightforward parts of the corpse, such as skeletons, skulls and bones, or the worms that always win in the end. Art and imagination have produced a Grim Reaper with a scythe, as well as a range of less frightening objects such as an hour-glass whose time has run out, a crumbling column with no building to support, or the broken spade a labourer will no longer need. A suitable background was provided by sadly drooping willows, a melancholy owl against a dying moon, or silently flitting bats – black, of course.

Black, with its traditional association with gloom, sombre spirits, the darkness of night and the inside of the tomb, has been the customary mourning shade for men in Britain since the fourteenth century. It was also worn by bereaved ancient Greeks and Romans, and most modern Europeans and Americans wear it to mark their sadness and respect.

But, because we are accustomed to it, we tend to forget that black has not always been the universal mourning colour – nor

14

is it even now. White, for example, is still popular for funerals in China. It has often been used for women and children to suggest virginity and innocence, and was worn by women in ancient Rome and Sparta, and in Spain until the fifteenth century. At Richard II's funeral in 1399 the thirty torch-bearers wore white. In 1536 Henry VIII wore white for mourning after Anne Boleyn was beheaded. And Queen Victoria had a white funeral. In some districts of Britain and the United States, long white silk hatbands flowed almost to the ground when the deceased was a child or unmarried.

Many South Sea islanders wear both black and white stripes so that the contrast expresses hope as well as sadness.

In Ethiopia the appropriate colour for mourning is considered to be the greyish brown of the earth to which the dead return, but mourners in Iran prefer the paler browns of withered leaves. Deep blue is the favourite in Turkestan, while Armenians and Syrians choose a blue of a lighter shade because it suggests to them the sky and the heavens beyond it.

At some periods purple and violet have been used for royalty and churchmen, or as an intermediate stage in mourning after unrelieved black, and sometimes the mourning colour for Very Important People in the Middle Ages was scarlet.

Visitors to Burma and the Far East will know that in some areas yellow predominates as a colour of mourning; it also used to be popular in Egypt and Brittany.

And in many areas, notably among the negroes in New Orleans, a funeral is not complete without groups of people in their brightest clothes, who dance to a band on their way to the cemetery to show their joy that their late friend has gone to a better world.

Other national customs and beliefs concerning death are as varied as life itself.

In China it is important for the deceased to have reached an advanced age, as the older he is the more important he is in the underworld. His relatives thus sometimes add several years to his age during childhood and several more when he dies. Therefore it is almost impossible to know exactly how long a person has lived. To the Chinese it is also very important to be buried well, so the family buys the most expensive coffin it can afford – often twenty years before it is needed.

Certain villages in Mexico still celebrate a folk belief known as The Day of the Dead. This holds that the souls of the dead return on two days each year – children on the first day of November and adults on the second. Offerings to welcome the returning soul include incense to guide it to its former home, a candle to light its way, water in case it is thirsty, flowers in its honour and food in case it is hungry. On the island of Janitzio in the Lake of Patzcuaro there is a *fiesta* for the dead, in which holy processions include treasured figures wearing velvet and with real hair. Bread is baked and eaten in the shapes of animals and people, and sweets are made like skulls. Also somewhat macabre, to European eyes, are cardboard coffins from which a skeleton pops up when you pull a string. (But the Mexican Embassy in London assures me that the Day of the Dead is now rarely celebrated and that the *fiesta* is now only a tourist attraction.) After a death, even the poorest families hold a wake around the body. Visitors give what they can, even if only a few coins, for the funeral. Sometimes powered lime is placed underneath the coffin for the good of the soul and a pot of vinegar with chopped onion, to help ward off disease.

In the country districts of Japan it is customary for the friends, relatives, neighbours and even acquaintances of the deceased's family to offer *koden* (incense money) to pay for the incense burned for the dead. A sum of money wrapped up in a formal manner, it derives from the custom of giving mutual help in times of need. As in the case of all the other gifts brought – like flowers, fruit and cakes – *okaeshi* (a return present) must be given for each *koden*. In some districts this is a special kind of sweet cake, while those city dwellers who still carry on the custom give a box of green tea.

The Japanese believe that for forty-nine days the spirit of the dead person is still under the roof of its earthly home. So on the forty-ninth day the family gathers to give it a farewell. This ceremony is carried out not with sorrow but with gladness because the deceased is now considered to be in paradise. Only now can his personal effects – such as kimonos, books, watches, furniture, pens, jewellery, pipes and walking-sticks – be touched. They are distributed among the family, friends, relations and servants. No one must be forgotten, and the selection must be made according to the degree of intimacy each had with the deceased. This can lead to bitter arguments as everyone wants the most valuable mementoes. Often he has too few possessions to go round, and neighbours or friends who have been ignored feel resentful. Arbitration in these disputes is supplied by the closest relatives.

The long black hair which was the pride of Japanese women until the late nineteenth century used to be cut short by widows, to show that they had no desire to marry again and were staying faithful to their late husbands. However, the widow had to get official permission from the local government office to cut her hair. She would receive a notice saying: 'The husband is dead, and his widow can cut her hair short. It cannot be said that she has no reason for making her hair short. Thus she will be allowed to do so.' If she had cut her hair without this reason she would be fined.

Widows would call themselves *mibojin,* meaning 'a person who has not yet died'. Man and wife were considered to be so inseparable that when he died she did too, spiritually, and her sense of devotion might even make her think of killing herself to follow her mate. If the husband died first his tombstone often bore her name as well as his own, as they were expected to be buried together. Among old-fashioned Japanese there still exists a feudalistic disapproval of widows remarrying. To enable widows to do so, there is now a movement to abolish the *mibojin* custom.

The happiness of the spirit of the dead in the afterworld depends largely upon the prayers and offerings made by the Japanese family and friends left behind. Among the services held are those for the repose of dead fish, eels and animals, which have been sacrificed for the livelihood or comfort of human beings. Children hold services for dolls they have broken in the past year. At the all-night watch over the dead there are prayers and discussions about the deceased's virtues, faults, mistakes, successes, habits and manners. It is an evening to remember the dead, with eating and drinking. This is believed to show respect, and the merrier the party the more satisfied are the bereaved relatives.

The more superstitious country people in Ireland cross themselves at the sight of a bird perched on the window-sill of a sick-room, or a raven flying over the house, or at the sound of a dog howling outside at night, for these are supposed to herald the approach of death. There used to be a tradition that a dying person's soul should be helped on its way to another existence, even if this meant knocking holes in walls or roofs. And, in case among the feathers in his mattress was one from a wild bird fighting to cling to life, he was taken from his bed and put outside to die.

After it was all over his bed was burned, the clocks were stopped and the mirrors veiled. The dead man's bees would know the worst when the hive was covered with a piece of crape. At the wake the visitors paid their respects, then shared food and drink, making sure the body was never left alone. Wakes were often lively affairs, with songs, music, dancing and stories. Sometimes a wild party developed, in fear that the deceased was envious of those who had survived and might be eager to take revenge on the successors to his property. But the Church frowned on wakes, and they are now rarer and more subdued.

Another Irish custom that has all but disappeared is 'keening' (lamenting for the dead). Women, as if in a trance, chanted dirges like :

The girls of the mountain may cry
By the running streams
For the flower of the country,
But he will return no more.

Close relatives naturally wept over the body, and again during the wake, but in addition men and women were hired to compose eulogies over the dead, accompanied by artificial wailing. This practice was general until the end of the nineteenth century, and was then strongly discouraged by the clergy.

Jews throughout the world observe a period of seven days' mourning after the burial, and for a certain number of weeks are required to give a prescribed oration during services at Orthodox synagogues. In Israel, burial is carried out by a special non-commercial society. A tombstone may not be laid until a month after the burial.

For Hindus, Buddhists and followers of some other religions in India, death is not an end. They believe implicitly in the law of *karma*, which stipulates that each individual passes through a series of lives. The conditions into which a man was born depended on his conduct in previous existences, and his attitude and behaviour in this life will greatly affect his reincarnation in the next. He actually looks forward to the next stage in the sequence, because through his personal efforts he may progress to ultimate bliss (*nirvana*). This is the 'Supreme State' of freedom from the cycle of birth and death called 'The Wandering', and is only achieved after a series of existences. Together with Buddhists, Brahmins believe that this present universe is neither the first nor the last. They would accept the doctrine that 'as a tree falls so shall it lie', but they deny it so lies for ever.

Parsees believe that the soul remains near the world for three days, so there are prayers and ceremonies for three days and nights. The body is never placed with the head pointing towards the north, and in all Parsee ceremonies the north side is avoided. This custom stems from the ancient Iranians, ancestors of the

Parsees, who believed the Spirit of Destruction flew in from the north in the form of a fly. Bandits, too, came ravaging from the north. Even the north wind was believed to be dangerous, striking with sickness and death.

Meticulous care is taken by Parsees over the disposal of the body, being careful to show all possible respect for it, as well as love and gratitude for the person who has gone, while at the same time demonstrating solicitude for the health of the living. Everything is thoroughly washed, including the shroud. This is usually white and made of cotton. It need not be new. In fact, old clothes are encouraged because it is forbidden that the body's disposal should involve wastage of clothes. Then the body is exposed, so as to attract flesh-devouring birds, on 'Towers of Silence'. These are made of stone, and usually set on a hill. Within two hours the corpse is completely stripped of flesh by the vultures, and the bones are thrown into a pit containing lime or phosphorus. In this way the Parsees combine their religious tradition with modern concern for hygiene, at the same time symbolizing the levelling aspect of death: 'Naked we come into this world and naked we leave it'.

The Muslims in Jordan have a totally different view on this method of disposal. A dead man must be buried the day he dies. Only if he dies in the evening may he be buried the next morning. It horrifies Arabs to think that a body is to be left above ground all night, and they keep watch by it because, they say, 'He must never be left alone. Birds and animals might touch him'.

The Arabs also believe that death is preferable on a Friday, as that is the Muslims' special day of prayer. And they have a saying: 'He who dies in Ramadan, the Month of Fasting, may be sure of entering Paradise. He will be released from torment and examinations'.

In Bali, when a tall bamboo pole by the gate of a house displays a bird and a swinging lamp – both made out of white paper – it means that a death has occurred. Balinese coffins are made in the shapes of animals, and there are tall towers of wood and bamboo, paper and silk. The decorations are cheerful, with bright ribbons and tinsel mirrors, because death is seen, again, as the liberation of the soul into better worlds. The funeral is an occasion for much eating and drinking.

In the Celebes, there is sometimes a gap of four years between the death of a great man and the disposal of his body. This gives time for the relatives to save up enough for a splendid festival which sometimes lasts several days. For a nobleman, sacrifices often include hundreds of buffaloes and pigs. Relatives from hundreds of miles around attend, and the more of these sacrificial animals they bring with them, the greater will be their share of the dead man's property.

In nomadic primitive societies that depended for their survival on hunting or herding it was accepted that when aged people could no longer play an active part their value to the tribe had declined and they had to be left to die. When the Omaha Indians moved camp they left any very old people behind, with shelter, food, water and a fire. A similar intensely practical attitude prevailed among the Eskimos, Lapps, Bushmen, Ainu and Australian Aborigines. In some societies the elderly have even made their own decision to die, becoming personally involved in the arrangements. In Samoa a sick old chief would ask to be buried alive, and if this request wasn't granted his family was disgraced.

The death of a patriarch has often been important to the tribe and its history. The death of a child is a sad event, but as an old man who has had a full and satisfying life nears death he is increasingly venerated. When an old Maori died there were always public celebrations to mark his death; his final blessings and curses were heard with much respect and his last words were considered highly significant. (There is an interesting analogy here with the general fascination for the last words spoken by the victims of public executions in England, in the days when highwaymen or sheep-stealers were hanged. It has been said that one of the main reasons for these affairs being so well attended was not simply the macabre fascination of the execution itself, but the fact that above all the populace wanted the criminal to say something just before he died. The finality of those words seemed to lend a sort of magic to the villain's last expressed thoughts on his life.)

To a Tibetan the Art of Dying, already referred to in Chapter 1, is linked with his belief in an intermediate state of forty-nine days' duration between life and death, known as *bardo*. The forms, rituals and ceremonies carried out during that period must be carefully controlled. If the complicated series of prayers and services are not followed exactly as laid down, the future of the deceased will be in peril.

Tibetans point out that the fear and morbidity which are evoked by death in the West, and the unwillingness to face it with understanding, are due to the emphasis people lay on the physical body, and their identification with it. There is also the fear of loneliness and the loss of the familiar. Yet the loneliness of death, when a man finds he is without a body, is as nothing compared to the loneliness of birth. At birth, the soul is in new surroundings, immersed in a body which is at first totally incompetent to take care of itself or to establish intelligent contact with its new world. It takes a long time before this loneliness disappears. After death, say the Tibetans, the dead man is never alone because he meets all those whom he knew during his physical life. He is also conscious of those still in physical bodies; he can see them and share their emotions and their thinking. A Tibetan lama has written : 'We all have died many deaths, before we came into this incarnation. And what we call birth is merely the reverse side of death, like one of the two sides of a coin, or like a door which we call "entrance" from outside and "exit" from inside a room'.

> Every stage of human life, except
> the last, is marked out by certain
> and defined limits; old age alone
> has no precise and determinate
> boundary.
>
> CICERO

Life-Spans and Expectations

Claims for longevity have been the subject of exaggeration and poetic licence since the time of Methuselah, who was said to have died at the age of 969. Although the more fanciful ones should therefore be greeted with scepticism – like that of the Arab who recently said he was 192, presumably to please the interviewer – it is known that groups of people in certain parts of the world – Ecuador, Russian Georgia and Pakistan, for example – still appear to exceed the generally expected life-span. And some rural districts of England and France are said to produce a regular crop of nonagenarians and centenarians.

Although the reasons for exceptionally long life have been variously attributed to climate, diet, and the absence of worry (deafness allegedly helping the latter), they cannot be established with certainty. Studies have shown that the children of long-lived parents tend to live longer than those of short-lived ones. Thus longevity may to some extent be determined by heredity.

Another likely determining factor is environment. In the past, adverse conditions reduced most people's years to far fewer than their possible span. Our prehistoric ancestors are thought to have died at an average age of seventeen, usually as the result of violence. An ancient Roman did not have much chance of living beyond his late twenties, and in eighteenth-century Britain the average expectation of life was still less than twenty-nine years.

In more recent times crowded living conditions, poor hygiene, epidemic diseases and inadequate diet also played their part in shortening people's lives. In Manchester in 1840 it was found that over 57 per cent of working-class children died before they reached the age of five; and in London in the 1830s the average age at death was said to be only twenty-two for 'labourers', twenty-five for 'tradesmen' (including clerks and their wives and children), but forty-four for the 'gentry'.

Precise measurements of human longevity and statistically reliable assessments of life expectancy have only become possible since the introduction of comprehensive registration of births and deaths (with dates and causes of death). In the United Kingdom this was inaugurated by the Births and Deaths Registration Act of 1836.

Fortunately, however, it has been possible to authenticate earlier records to establish the greatest age to which a human being has ever been known to live. This distinction was achieved by Pierre Joubert, a French-Canadian, who died in Quebec in 1814, aged 113 years and 124 days. The oldest authenticated age for a woman appears to be 112 years 39 days, achieved as recently as 1973 by a British woman, Alice Stevenson.

Naturally one marvels at these rare achievements, but more relevant to this book is the question of life expectancy for the ordinary person.

In general terms the chance of dying at any given age is greater for men than for women. It is high during the first year after birth, reaches its lowest point during childhood, and increases more rapidly with advancing age.

To put this into a more practical perspective, statisticians use the measure of *expectation of life*. This is calculated from statistics of past deaths among the appropriate section of the population, and is defined officially as 'the average future lifetime which would be lived, if subject to normal death probabilities'. This figure forms a basis for countless other calculations, from population forecasts to life insurance premiums.

For purposes of comparison with other times or with other countries, the most significant expectation-of-life figure is that for newly-born babies, known as *initial life expectancy*. In Britain in 1840, when the first reliable official tables were published, it was only forty years for boys and forty-two years for girls. By 1901 it had risen, but only to 48.1 years and 51.8 years respectively.

During the next sixty years initial life expectancy improved steadily by about three years in each decade, so that in 1961 a newly-born boy could expect to live for 67.9 years and a girl for 73.8 years. Since then, the conditions favouring greater expectations seem to have reached a plateau (at least for the present), and the increase in initial expectancy has levelled out almost entirely. According to 1971 figures, the latest available, it is now 68.6 years for boys and 74.9 years for girls. Yet as recently as 1970 the initial expectancy for baby boys in the African republic of Gabon was still only about twenty-five years.

An important factor in this improvement has been the dramatic decrease in infant mortality (death during the first year after birth). Around 1901, of every 1,000 live births of each sex, 185 boys and 147 girls died before their first birthday, or about seventeen babies in every hundred. By 1973 the rate had fallen to only nineteen boys and fifteen girls per 1,000, or fewer than two babies in every hundred.

For girls, another factor contributing to longer life expectancy has been the reduction in their chances of dying during pregnancy or childbirth. Around 1901, for every 100,000 babies born alive, 471 mothers gave their own lives. By 1945 this maternal death rate had dropped to 199 per 100,000, still a substantial figure. But in 1972 it was only fifteen per 100,000 – a remarkable testimonial to modern medical treatment.

From this initial starting point, the age to which one can expect to live increases as one grows older. In a sense, initial life expectancy represents a 'basic ration' with which we are all equipped at the start of our lives. Thereafter, on every birthday from the first onwards, one is given – statistically speaking – 'bonuses' of additional expectancy, earned as rewards for surviving the constant hazards of human existence. This principle extends throughout the entire human life-span. Even centenarians, who have long ago exceeded their initial expectancy, can expect to live for some two more years. If they do, still further (but always a little smaller) leases of expected life await them.

The following table, based on 1960-62 figures, demonstrates this principle among people of different ages.

Age reached	*Age to which expected to live*	
	MALES	FEMALES
Birth	68.1	74.0
5 years	70.1	75.7
10 years	70.2	75.8
20 years	70.6	76.0
30 years	71.1	76.2
40 years	71.6	76.7
50 years	72.7	77.6
60 years	75.1	79.1
70 years	79.3	81.8
80 years	85.2	86.4
90 years	93.0	93.3
95 years	97.4	97.5
100 years	102.0	102.0

Some interesting points emerge from this table. First, note how women's greater life expectancy – by nearly six years initially – persists through all ages until only at 100 is it finally matched by men. One can also see how the 'bonuses' of life expectancy rise to a peak in older age, for those who have proved their above-average capacity for survival.

But probably the most surprising fact emerges when these modern expectancies are compared with those of 1900. Although initial life expectancy has increased greatly, and expectancy among middle age-groups has also increased, there has been hardly any improvement in life expectancy for older people, particularly men. In 1901, a man who survived to seventy could expect to live to 78.4 years. But even today the expectancy of a seventy year old man is only about one year higher, at 79.4 years. The difference is even less for male octogenarians, with expectancies then and now of 84.9 and 85.5 years.

Among women, there has been some progress. Where the expectancy of a woman of seventy in 1901 was 79.2 years, it is now nearly three years higher at 82.4 years.

Sir Peter Medawar, the immunologist and specialist in ageing, has commented on this in an interview reported in *The Times*: 'Little advance has been made recently in prolonging the life-span, but that is not surprising. In former days a person who reached the age of sixty had to have been pretty tough – natural selection had been operating throughout life and the weaker would have fallen. There is no God-given parameter called the normal life-span; the life-span is what we cause it to be. Life-span can be prolonged in mice and rats, but only by using means which it is not easy to see as applicable to man. If a method were devised to prolong the span then our conception of the right and proper age to die would change accordingly.'

Although people may not be living much longer overall, however, there are now very many more long-lived people. Indeed since 1901 the entire 'shape' of the population has changed. In the nineteenth century death took its toll fairly evenly through all ages, resulting in a population whose numbers, in successive age groups, formed an almost regular 'pyramid', with only about 6 per cent surviving to sixty-five years or more.

Today the pyramid has become much more barrel-shaped. The actual number of people in younger age-groups is little different from that in 1901; but the proportion of the population above the age of thirty has grown dramatically. In 1973, 10.6 per cent of all men were over sixty-five, and 22 per cent of all women were aged sixty or more. And while in 1901 only 500,000 people were aged seventy-five and over, by 1972 the number had risen to 2,600,000 – with a forecast of $3\frac{1}{2}$ million by the year 2001.

Sex and age structure of the population
United Kingdom

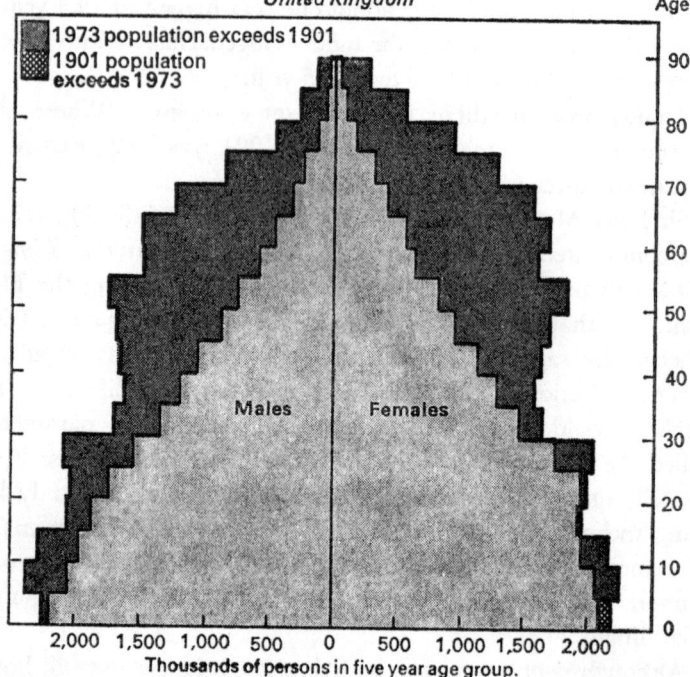

SOURCE: *Social Trends No. 4, 1973.*

Causes of Death

Modern statistics on the causes of death lack the sense of drama that characterized their earlier counterparts. The following extract from an analysis of local deaths in the 'Weekly Bill of Mortality' was printed in the first issue of the *Reading Mercury* in 1723:

Apoplexy	3
Asthma	1
Colick	4

Consumption	56
Stoppage i' th' Stomach	3
Mortification	5
Suddenly	1
Cut his throat at St Giles without Cripplegate	1
Drownded	2
Excessive drinking	1
Poisoned herself at St Brides	1

And the year 1657 was evidently a busy time for a Dr Heberden, in London, who compiled this list:

Flox and Small Pox	835
Found dead in the streets, etc.	9
French Pox	25
Gout	8
Griefe	10
Griping and Plague in the Guts	446
Hang'd and made away 'emselves	24

Although the term 'Griefe' suggests that ten people pined away of sheer sorrow, Dr Heberden probably used it in one of the senses recorded by the *Oxford English Dictionary* as in use in the early eighteenth century, i.e. 'a sore, wound; a blemish of the skin; a disease, sickness'.

Today the *Registrar General's Statistical Review,* and the associated analyses of social trends, provide far more detailed and precise information on Britain's population and mortality. Almost all the figures quoted in this chapter come from these sources – and here it must be pointed out that while some of these relate, strictly speaking, to 'England and Wales', others relate to the 'United Kingdom'. For the sake of simplicity, however, we have ignored variations and quoted all figures as applying, in the most general sense, to 'Britain'.

Causes of death listed in the *Statistical Review* follow the International Classification of Diseases, with 1,000 categories. These include 800 'medical' categories, many with sub-divisions, in sections ranging from 'Infective and Parasitic Diseases' and 'Neoplasms' to 'Diseases of the Musculoskeletal System and Connective Tissue' and a final gathering of 'Symptoms and Ill-Defined Conditions'. After these come 200 categories of 'Accidents, Poisoning and Violence', classified by the nature of the external cause, and also by the resultant injury.

Just as the moment of death can be defined in many ways, the term 'cause of death' is open to differing interpretations, especially when comparing data from different countries. As the *Review* says: 'it must be emphasised that there are significant variations in methods and efficiency of diagnosing, naming, registering and certifying causes of death'. Since 1953 the World Health Organization has recommended that records are based on the concept of the *underlying cause of death,* rather than the ultimate cause closest to death itself, and this is defined as 'the disease or injury which initiated the train of morbid events leading directly to death, or . . . the circumstances of the accident or violence which produced the fatal injury'.

By far the commonest cause of death in Britain today – as in many other parts of the world – is ischaemic heart disease. This term embraces all the conditions in which the heart fails for lack of blood, including coronary thrombosis (formation of a blood clot) and atheroma (narrowing of coronary arteries). In 1972 it accounted for a quarter of all deaths in Britain, striking particularly at men from their mid-thirties onwards. Among women it is also the major cause of death, although the numbers it claims are notably fewer (72,000 in 1972 against 98,000 men), and its greatest effect is in later age, among the over-sixties.

Indeed at a medical conference in 1975, it was said that thrombosis is affecting society 'like the rat-borne plagues of the Middle Ages'; that its high incidence accounts for the virtually static average life expectancy of British men; and that, in Holland, male life expectancy is now even dropping.

The variation in incidence among men and women is characteristic of all major causes of death.

Percentage of total deaths, 1972

CAUSE	MALES	FEMALES	ALL
Ischaemic heart disease	29.4	22.4	25.98
Cerebrovascular disease ('stroke')	10.8	17.43	14.06
Cancer (all kinds)	21.38	18.72	20.07
Bronchitis	7.1	2.61	4.88
Pneumonia (except new-born)	6.4	8.35	7.38
Accidents (motor and other)	3.3	2.77	3.07

Taken together, these six main categories account for about 75 per cent of all deaths in Britain. The figures show that while proportionally more males die from heart disease and bronchitis, and to some extent cancer, females are notably more susceptible to strokes. But the greatest differences are within the figures for cancer. In 1972, more than four times as many males (28,624) died of lung and respiratory cancer than females (6,608). It accounted for more than half of all male cancer deaths, but for only 15 per cent of those among women. And even if female deaths from cancer of the breast (12,299) and cervix (2,430) are included, the total is still far fewer than male deaths from lung cancer alone.

In *The British Journal of Surgery* for January 1975, Lord Brock, the former President of the Royal College of Surgeons, stated that this high mortality from lung cancer is due simply to the large proportions of patients whose disease is too advanced for operative treatment when they are first seen by the surgeon. When operation is possible, many patients can be completely cured and survive in good health for many years.

The table below shows the number and proportion of deaths in all the principal categories.

Deaths by principal categories: Great Britain 1972

	MALES		FEMALES		ALL PERSONS:
	Number of deaths in 1972	*%*	*Number of deaths in 1972*	*%*	*percentage of total deaths 1972*
Tuberculosis, respiratory	1,106	0.33	387	0.12	0.23
Tuberculosis, other	86	0.03	118	0.04	0.03
Syphilis and other venereal disease	92	0.03	68	0.02	0.02
Meningococcal infections	100	0.03	57	0.02	0.02
Acute poliomyelitis including late effects	7	—	10	—	—
Cancer:					
Digestive system	22,450	6.72	21,413	6.62	6.67
Lung, bronchus, trachea	28,624	8.58	6,608	2.04	5.36
Breast	88	0.03	12,299	3.80	1.89
Cervix uteri	—	—	2,430	0.75	0.37
Leukaemia	1,797	0.54	1,630	0.50	0.52
Other cancers	18,405	5.51	16,168	5.00	5.26
Diabetes	2,189	0.66	3,829	1.18	0.92
Cerebrovascular disease	35,965	10.78	56,379	17.44	14.06
Chronic rheumatic heart disease	2,624	0.79	4,645	1.44	1.11
Hypertensive heart disease	4,414	1.32	5,600	1.73	1.52
Ischaemic heart disease	98,245	29.45	72,442	22.41	25.98
Influenza	1,612	0.48	1,818	0.56	0.52
Pneumonia (except new-born)	21,455	6.43	27,001	8.35	7.38
Bronchitis	23,634	7.08	8,450	2.61	4.88
Ulcer of stomach	908	0.27	868	0.27	0.27
Ulcer of duodenum	1,470	0.44	681	0.21	0.33
Nephritis and nephrosis	1,588	0.48	1,404	0.43	0.46
Hyperplasia of prostate	1,347	0.40	—	—	0.21
Pregnancy, childbirth, abortion	—	—	125	0.04	0.02
Congenital malformations	2,465	0.74	2,418	0.75	0.74
Motor vehicle accidents	5,284	1.58	2,513	0.78	1.19
All other accidents	5,882	1.76	6,464	2.00	1.88
Suicide and self-inflicted injury	2,436	0.73	1,755	0.54	0.64
Other causes	49,376	14.80	65,722	20.32	17.52
All causes	333,604		323,302		

SOURCE: *Social Trends.*

It can be seen above that some widely fatal diseases of past ages now barely exist in the statistics. Of a total of nearly 657,000 deaths in 1972, respiratory tuberculosis claimed only 1,493 – fewer than half the total ten years previously. And poliomyelitis, the cause of several hundred deaths per year in the early 1950s, has been virtually eradicated, with only 17 deaths. Influenza, which took as many as 112,000 lives in Britain during the world epidemic of 1918, is also much less to be feared, although its incidence still varies considerably from year to year (3,430 deaths in 1972, but only 746 in 1971).

Causes of death also vary greatly between different age groups. The chart on page 34 gives causes of death in 1972 in the centre column, with their relative incidence among males and females shown in bars on either side.

Up to one year, Nature seems to be selecting the fittest of the new-born. Indeed, as shown by the circled figures, the death rate among this group is greater than at any succeeding time until late middle age. The main hazards are 'perinatal' causes – those occurring at birth and shortly afterwards – consisting of various conditions affecting breathing, blood circulation and other essential functions. Congenital malformations also take a substantial (and probably often merciful) toll.

Among those aged one to fourteen years the incidence of deaths is at its lowest, reaching the minimum among those aged between ten and fourteen years; but the variety of causes is comparatively large. Over 40 per cent of all accidental deaths from drowning occur among this age group. Motor accidents make their first significant appearance, and so does cancer.

Between the ages fifteen to thirty-four, motor accidents overshadow all other single causes of death among men, while cancer becomes the greatest single hazard for women. And it is here that suicide makes its only substantial showing.

Beyond thirty-five, the two main overall causes of death – heart disease and cancer – take the lead among men and women respectively. And much the same pattern continues for the re-

Principal causes of death for each age group, 1972

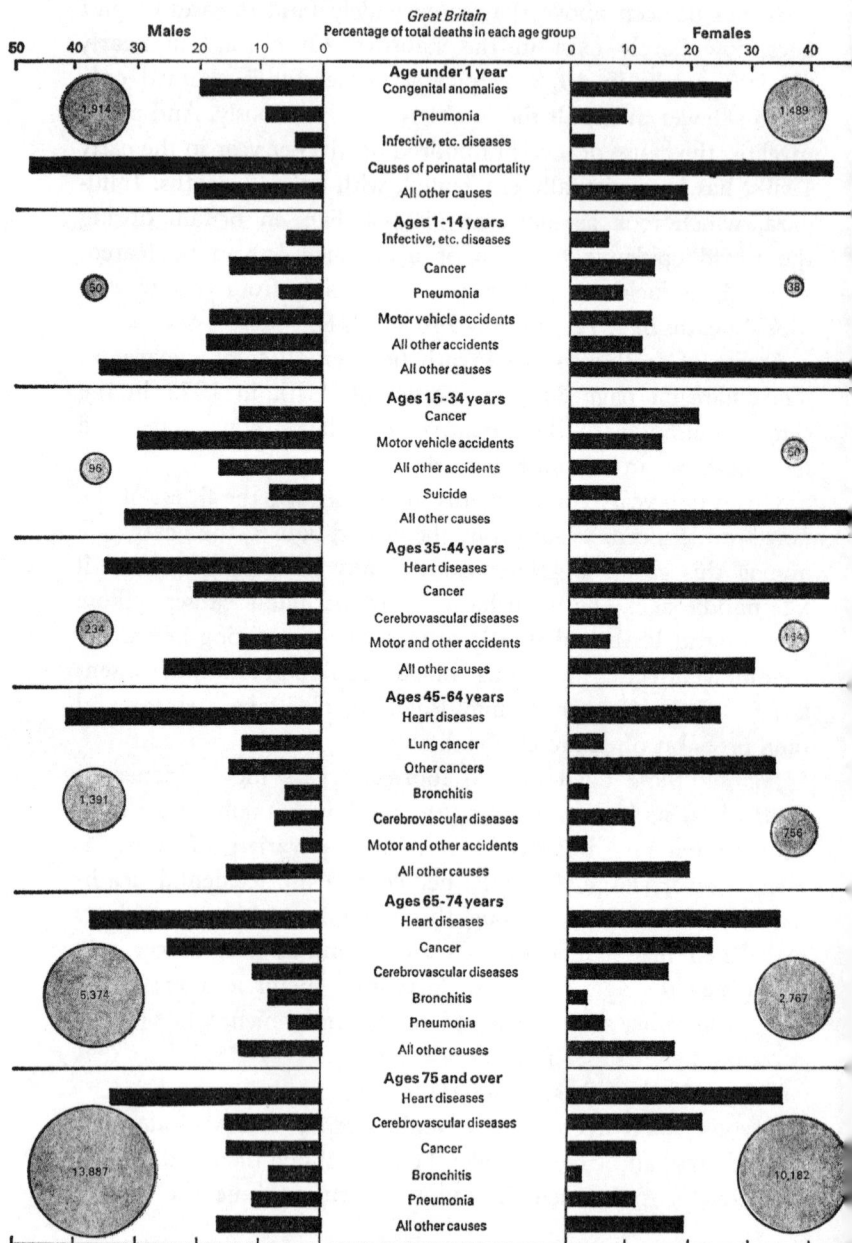

Great Britain
Percentage of total deaths in each age group

| Males | | Females |
| 50 40 30 20 10 0 | | 0 10 20 30 40 |

Age under 1 year
Congenital anomalies
Pneumonia
Infective, etc. diseases
Causes of perinatal mortality
All other causes

Ages 1-14 years
Infective, etc. diseases
Cancer
Pneumonia
Motor vehicle accidents
All other accidents
All other causes

Ages 15-34 years
Cancer
Motor vehicle accidents
All other accidents
Suicide
All other causes

Ages 35-44 years
Heart diseases
Cancer
Cerebrovascular diseases
Motor and other accidents
All other causes

Ages 45-64 years
Heart diseases
Lung cancer
Other cancers
Bronchitis
Cerebrovascular diseases
Motor and other accidents
All other causes

Ages 65-74 years
Heart diseases
Cancer
Cerebrovascular diseases
Bronchitis
Pneumonia
All other causes

Ages 75 and over
Heart diseases
Cerebrovascular diseases
Cancer
Bronchitis
Pneumonia
All other causes

Figures in circles represent the death rate from *all* causes in 1972-per 100,000 population in each age and sex group.

SOURCE: *Social Trends No. 4, 1973.*

mainder of the human life-span, except in the over-seventy-five group, where the proportion of cancer deaths tails off to some extent and the incidence of cerebrovascular diseases reaches its peak.

Finally, one may note among the less widespread causes of death that between 1961 and 1972 nobody died of ratbite fever or yaws; that psittacosis (parrot disease) claimed five lives while bunions allegedly killed twenty-four; that execution (no cases since 1964) is classified as a form of 'legal intervention'; that lightning claimed from one to eleven victims in each year; and that one person is recorded to have died of flat feet.

> Science says 'We must live', and seeks
> the means of prolonging, increasing,
> facilitating and amplifying life, of
> making it tolerable and acceptable;
> wisdom says 'We must die', and seeks
> how to make us die well.
>
> MIGUEL DE UNAMUNO

Ageing and Death

The rate of ageing differs little from person to person; the odds on dying between the ages of sixty-five and eighty are very high. But a man is not quite like a watch running down, for a man can repair himself; yet, once run down, he cannot be rewound. Vigour diminishes with age, so that an illness mild in youth may topple an old man into the grave. There is less adaptation to environmental change and less resilience.

What are the factors that affect the ageing process? There is heredity: long-lived parents tend to have long-lived children, and brevity of life is also handed down. Sex is important: women live on average five years longer than men. The married live longer than the single, because they look after each other and marriage is psychologically healthier than celibacy. Clergymen live long, perhaps because they are half-starved and have no motorcars! An excess of brain-tissue over what is to be expected in relation to body-weight is also correlated with longevity. The hormones change with age; but hormone treatment cannot reverse or postpone senescence. Ionizing radiation is often thought to accelerate the ageing process; and we are all subject to cosmic radiations, X-rays and the effects of atomic explosions.

Simple animals in whom cell-growth continues to replace cell for cell seem to be immune from the ageing process and may live for ever, barring accidents. But cells which are no longer able to divide have limited lives; human nerve cells never divide, once formed, and this sets a limit to their operational life. Senescence may therefore be due to loss of cells that cannot be replaced; but it may also be that the cells produced in later life are less fit than those produced in youth. The body, which appears so static, is in fact in a process of continuous self-renewal; but the cells produced in old age tend to undergo changes, or mutations, which make the body less and less a true copy of itself; they may become independent and cancerous, there are changes in cell chemistry and the information-carrying power of the chromosomes. The very intercellular ground-substance of the tissues may degenerate.

More philosophically, there is a failure of guidance and control mechanisms in age; we run out of evolutionary programming. We are, as it were, shot into life with a certain impetus that will theoretically drive us on for a span of seventy to eighty years. But whether we attain this age depends on the resistance encountered as we move through life – on disease, injury and the increasing loss of capacity for self-repair. One of the few verified factors known to prolong life is undernourishment during the growing period; this leads to a prolongation of immaturity and a postponement of the ageing process.

The Definition of Death

What is death? Perhaps we should first ask: What is life? Life is the synthesis of complex molecules from simpler materials into an integrated organized system which maintains itself like a whirlpool. It reverses the ordinary laws of thermodynamics. Energy is not dissipated, order is maintained in an increasingly disordered and cooling universe. To use another metaphor, life is like a gyroscope which, most improbably, stays upright so long as it spins above a minimum speed; life is an *improbability* in an only too predictable environment.

If life is taken as the persistence of certain reactions or behaviour patterns, then presumably the organism is dead when these are irretrievably lost. But the situation is not so clear-cut in organisms with a complex central nervous system, for this may be knocked out, the brain may die, responses cease, and yet other organs, even the body as a whole, may survive or be kept alive by artificial means. Life without a brain is an every-day hospital occurrence – but is this life, or death? Further, the integrated body may die, yet life continue in many of its cells and tissues. Cells may be kept growing and multiplying in culture in a flask for years, even decades, after the death of the body from which they came; conversely, certain organs may die long before the death of their owner.

Definitions of death range from the broadly scientific ('permanent cessation of the vital functions of the body') to the highly jargonized ('absolute dysfunction with zero transitional probability to a higher state'); from the chemical ('lack of ability to synthesize molecules in an integrated organized system') to the theological ('loss of spiritual life'). So death may mean many things and occur at many levels. Medically, we have molecular death (the death of cells), somatic death (that of the whole body), clinical death (cessation of breath and heartbeat) and the death of the brain (irreversible coma). More poetically, there is the death of the spirit and the death of the heart. Let us first deal with clinical death.

Once the heart stops beating the body cells are no longer being supplied with vital materials through the bloodstream. They will then die, for an irreversible chemical change will have taken place. But this does not happen immediately, or even simultaneously, for some tissues are more dependent on their blood-supply than others and have a shorter survival time. Brain cells die if deprived of oxygen for four minutes and even if the heart is restarted after this time, normal cerebral function will not return though the rest of the body survives. Within these critical four minutes, those whose hearts have stopped may –

sometimes – be restored to life by cardiac massage or electrical stimulation. After a longer period resuscitation of the body as a whole is impossible by any currently known means, and molecular death is inevitable.

But in the sense that an irreversible sequence of events has been initiated, death may also have begun long before this point. The tissues of vital organs may be invaded by tumours which cause local damage and interfere with general nutrition. Acute infections or poisoning can kill by damaging essential structures or by interfering with the metabolism at cell level. The lungs' vital function of transferring oxygen to the blood and removing carbon dioxide can be abolished by respiratory diseases, inhalation of noxious gases, or by drowning. Kidney damage or disease initiates a chain of biochemical events that may end in high blood-pressure, uraemia and death. The blockage of an important artery may progressively reduce or suddenly interrupt the blood-supply to some organ; if this is the brain, there is a stroke which may cause first unconsciousness, then death. Thus, disease of the arteries is an important contributor to death. Quite early in life, fatty material begins to be deposited in and under their smooth linings. They lose their patency and flexibility and slowly silt up. This is a gradual process; but a sudden total blockage may be produced by a superadded spasm or clotting, as in coronary thrombosis; or a damaged vessel in the brain may give way and cause a cerebral haemorrhage.

The Diagnosis of Death

Classically, death has occurred when heartbeat and breathing have stopped. But clinically this is not always easy to determine, for in deep coma or after certain forms of poisoning, breathing may be so shallow as to be undetectable. No haze appears on a mirror held at the mouth, and the pulse may be so feeble as to be undetectable at the wrist or even by a stethoscope over the heart.

Certain other clinical features may be helpful in such cases. At death, the facial muscles relax and sag; the eyes stare; the skin of the finger-webs loses its pink transparency. After death, if the skin is blanched by pressure, the colour does not readily return; it will not respond to burning by reddening or blistering; and no bleeding issues from a trial incision.

Obviously, in cases of doubt additional techniques are helpful, such as electrocardiographic records of heart action. Evidence of *brain* death, as distinct from total *body* death, is also important, especially when life is being artificially maintained in a respirator. The criteria laid down by the Harvard Medical School are as follows : The patient is quite unaware and unresponsive. Stimuli normally painful do not cause groaning, limb withdrawal or deeper or faster breathing; and no such responses to stimulation occur over an hour's observation. The pupils are fixed and dilated and do not respond to bright light. There are no eye movements when the head is turned to one side or the ears irrigated with ice-water. The tendon reflexes are absent. If the patient is in a respirator and this is switched off, there are no spontaneous efforts at breathing. The electroencephalogram is quite flat. All these tests should be repeated after twenty-four hours, but they may still be unreliable as indicators of irreversible brain damage when there is hypothermia (body temperature below 90°F or 32.2°C due to exposure) or in depression of the central nervous system from barbiturate poisoning.

Mistakes in the certification of death have been made since the earliest times and doctors make no claim to infallibility in this respect. Numerous instances have been recorded where revival has occurred spontaneously in the mortuary, or even in the coffin, or after the stimulus of a commencing post-mortem examination. The enormous increase in recent years in attempted suicide by taking an overdose of drugs has increased the problem of certification, for such patients are in artificial hibernation with slowed metabolism and their respiration and heartbeat may be undetectable to clinical examination. A typical case is that of a woman of seventy-eight who was discovered apparently dead with an empty bottle of sleeping pills and a suicide note by her side. She was declared dead and taken to the mortuary, where she lay for six hours until the policeman who came to identify her found that she was still breathing. She was, in fact, merely in deep narcosis – 'suspended animation'. It may well be that the practice of mourners watching over the body while it awaits burial is due partly to the ever-present possibility of their detecting signs of life.

For the same reason, a mortuary in Frankfurt-am-Main was once equipped with strings tied to the corpse's fingers which would ring a bell if there was any movement. And a more elaborate apparatus was devised by a Russian court chamberlain who had been much disturbed by an incident during the funeral of a young girl: the earth was already covering the coffin when she woke from her trance and screamed. He planned to fix a long tube from the chest of the corpse to above ground-level. The least movement of the chest would release a spring causing light and air to flow into the coffin, a flag would wave, bells ring, and the victim's voice would be transmitted through the tube. More prosaic, but more efficient, is the argument of Dr Roger Chapman, Sheffield's Deputy Medical Officer of Health, who pointed out in 1970 that there would be fewer mistaken certifications of death if all mortuaries were equipped with cardiac oscilloscopes. Such a technique had already detected electrical impulses from the heart of a girl certified dead from an overdose and would help to eliminate the very real fear, in older people, of being taken to the mortuary before death has actually occurred.

Resuscitation

In earlier societies death was regarded as akin to sleep and corresponding methods were used to revive persons unconscious or dead: shouting, slapping, whipping, or burning with live embers. An Egyptian who fell into the Nile would be hung upside-down to drain the water from his lungs or rolled vigorously across a barrel or an ox. In the eighteenth century the apparently drowned were vigorously shaken and kept warm by being bedded between two other persons or buried in heated ashes; the would-be life-savers also had to contend with the fact that resuscitation of the drowned was considered, by popular superstition, to be extremely unlucky. The North American Indians used to blow bamboo smoke into the rectum in an attempt to arouse an apparently dead man. Before we smile too much at such barbarous ignorance, it is worth noting that in the eighteenth century our own Royal Humane Society devised an apparatus for inflating tobacco smoke or the effluvia of aromatic herbs into the lungs or bowels; the apparatus still exists and was exhibited at Brighton in 1970.

In more modern times, progress led to a clear distinction between artificial respiration and restarting the heart. The first is designed to keep the blood oxygenated in the lungs, the second to maintain a circulation of oxygenated blood to the brain and body. In some cases respiration has failed but the heart is still beating; in others both have come to a halt before resuscitation is attempted.

As far as artificial respiration is concerned, an early attempt was made by the sixteenth-century physician, Vesalius, who tried to blow air into the windpipe through a reed. With the growth of the various humane and first-aid societies in the eighteenth century, more efficient methods were evolved in which the arms were elevated and the ribs compressed. But most satisfactory is the present-day 'kiss of life' which seems to have come back to us from biblical times. To quote from the Book of Kings: 'Then he went up and lay upon the child, putting his mouth on his mouth, his eyes upon his eyes, and his hands upon his hands; and as he stretched himself upon him the flesh of the child became warm'.

Revival of heart action by frequent, vigorous compression

applied to the breastbone probably dates back a hundred years. It may be done anywhere, under any conditions, and does two things: it passively maintains an appreciable peripheral circulation by squeezing the heart, and it directly stimulates the heart muscle. It must be carried out seventy to eighty times a minute with the victim lying on his back on a firm surface, preferably the floor or the ground. Carried out too vigorously, there is a risk of rib fracture, especially in children, but this is a small price to pay for success. Sometimes a single-handed operator must combine external cardiac massage with mouth-to-mouth breathing, closing the nostrils with one hand while breathing into the mouth and compressing the chest with the other.

When cardiac arrest occurs in hospital, cardiac compression remains the initial method of choice but certain added techniques are also available. Injections of adrenalin or other agents can be given into the veins or into the heart itself. More important, electrical shocks may be applied to the heart via electrodes on the chest-wall. These may restore an arrested heart to normal activity, or they may produce a state of 'fibrillation' in which the ventricles quiver ineffectively, and the latter state can then be dealt with by further shocks and the injection of various drugs.

If cardiac arrest is to be dealt with effectively by electrical stimulation, certain requirements must be met. The hospital must have a cardiac arrest alarm system so that alerted physicians may repair speedily and without confusion, and with their apparatus, to the right spot. Pending their arrival efficient external cardiac compression must be maintained. The time of onset of the arrest must, if possible, be noted accurately; this is easy during an operation, for the anaesthetist is watching the pulse and there is a clock on the wall, but may be impossible when death occurs quietly in a hospital bed. The time is important because of the four-minute limit for survival of the brain cells. If the heart is restarted after this time there is a danger of decerebration which, at its worst, leaves a human vegetable who may need permanent life-support in a mechanical respirator.

Until recently, there was also a place for open heart massage. The chest was opened by incising between the ribs on the left side and the heart was then squeezed between the hands. This is not now normally practised if efficient external compression is applicable and if electrical stimulation is at hand, but may have to be resorted to under certain circumstances. Sometimes the heart sac is full of blood or the lungs have been injured and then it is safer to expose the heart directly. Sometimes no electrical stimulation is available within a reasonable time and external compression, though maintaining some circulation, does not succeed in restoring active contraction. If cardiac arrest occurs during an operation the surgeon may well be inclined, since the patient is already on the operating table and skilled help and instrumentation are at hand, to open the chest without delay; but, barring these circumstances, chest compression is the method of choice. A first-aid measure sometimes useful at the outset is to bang the chest or strike it a vigorous blow with a wet towel. But the important thing is that everyone concerned should be familiar with the drill for cardiac arrest and the need for urgency, and that a skilled resuscitation team with the requisite apparatus should be at hand within the vital four minutes. Using such techniques, an astonishingly high success-rate was reported in 1972 from the Montreal General Hospital. Over a ten-year period the team there attempted to restart the hearts of 1,204 dying patients. Of these 230 left the hospital alive; more than half of those so saved were alive three years later and more than a third after seven years. Only four of the survivors had any permanent brain damage.

The modern heroes of resuscitation stories are often ambulance men, for they are usually the first on the scene with any training and never abandon their efforts while any hope remains. Even in apparently hopeless cases, when persons have been buried in sand or suffered severe electric shock or immersion in freezing water or massive drug overdose, prolonged unremitting cardiac compression and perhaps the use of a lung-inflator have worked miracles. The most important first-aid measure in dealing with an unconscious person at the scene of an accident is to see that the airway is clear. The mouth should be emptied of blood, dirt or mucus, the tongue and lower jaw pulled forward, and the victim turned on his side or face. Then, with a clear airway, either natural breathing will resume or artificial respiration can be instituted.

Resuscitation after immersion presents certain problems because an apparently dead body recovered from cold water may in fact be a victim of hypothermia. Anyone who falls into cold water will lose consciousness as soon as his body temperature falls to 33°C. Even a fit man will do so within twenty minutes if the temperature of the water is below 5°C; and, surprisingly, all the more quickly if he struggles or tries to swim. A person recovered in such a state of hypothermia may display no signs of life even to trained observers, for the respiration and heart-beat may be virtually undetectable. This condition is the cause of many of the thousand-odd deaths from drowning that occur in Britain every year. A report from the Royal Society of Medicine in 1973 warned against trying to give artificial respiration or cardiac massage in such cases. Instead, the victim should be taken, wrapped in blankets or some other insulating covering, to where he can be immersed in a bath of warm water, the temperature of which is increased until the body temperature approaches normal levels. The re-warming should be fairly rapid. Attempts at active resuscitation before this is achieved may only irritate the dormant heart muscle. Persons known to have only just entered the water may be revived by the usual means; but in all other cases, as when a body is found wearing a life-jacket, the re-warming technique is essential.

A rather different field for resuscitation is that concerned with elderly feeble patients or persons with advanced malignant disease. Should one, for instance, try very hard, or at all, to revive a woman of ninety with multiple fractures who has been dying from broncho-pneumonia, or a patient with multiple secondary deposits from cancer? These deaths usually occur in a hospital bed, sometimes after an operation and in such cases there is often a tacit and unwritten understanding between doctors and nurses that resuscitation will not be attempted, a merciful form of negative euthanasia. There are of course borderline cases, the ethical problems are sometimes tricky, and the procedure can never be formalized; it is all rather a question of:

> Thou shalt not kill but needst not strive
> Officiously to keep alive.

THE DEAD BODY

We have noted above some of the classical signs indicating that a person has died: cessation of heartbeat and breathing, relaxation of facial muscles, staring eyes, and so on. There are other changes that take place after death which are useful in determining the time of death and, occasionally, the cause of death. These might be called the forensic aspects of death and are the province of the pathologist. It is his job to investigate the changes brought about in the body by disease, infection or injury – if necessary, carrying out an autopsy on the body to establish as far as possible the exact cause of death. He will also look at certain external features, such as unusual discoloration of the skin (e.g. the cherry-red of carbon monoxide poisoning), any marks of injury, or any signs inconsistent with the alleged time of death, such as well-marked cooling, rigor or hypostasis (see below) in a body alleged to have just died. The pathologist will be called in by the coroner, to whom deaths in a variety of circumstances – after accidents, suicides, criminal deaths, deaths in custody or after operations (see Chapter 6 for further details) – must be reported by doctors or the police. It is, of course, in cases of criminal deaths (murder, manslaughter and the like) that the work of the forensic pathologist is particularly important and most often comes to the public notice. In such cases, establishing the time of death is of the utmost importance.

The Time of Death

The rectal temperature falls by approximately one-half to two-thirds of a degree Centigrade an hour during the first few hours after death. This helps in establishing the time of death. But any estimate of the time of death can never be precise; it is always plus or minus two hours, a bracket of the possibilities. Cooling is affected by clothing, artificial warmth, the ambient temperature, body size and physique, and by the starting temperature at death, which is high in fever and low in cases of exposure.

Post-mortem staining (hypostasis, lividity): After death, the blood settles in the dependent parts and leaks into the tissues, i.e. in the ordinary supine position there is staining of the back of the trunk and limbs beginning within three to six hours after death. The stains resemble bruises. The colour of the staining may indicate various forms of poisoning. If the body has been moved after death, this may be indicated by staining in the uppermost parts which were formerly dependent. When staining does *not* occur, it indicates that the dead person either bled to death or was anaemic.

Rigor mortis is a stiffening due to changes in the muscle proteins brought about by acid breakdown products. It usually begins after six hours in the muscles of the eyelids and jaw and spreads to the larger groups of muscles. It is complete at twelve hours, persists for another twelve, and passes off in the succeeding twelve; i.e. it has disappeared thirty-six hours after death. But this timetable is very variable. Rigor sets in very rapidly if there has been violent exertion just before death, it is slight after death from prolonged illness and is often absent in children. Its onset is more rapid in hot weather and delayed by cold. It should not be confused with *cadaveric spasm,* which is an instantaneous

rigor occurring at death, usually as a clutching or grasping of
the hands at objects when falling. This has also been noticed
on the battlefield.

Decomposition : The time of onset of actual decomposition
varies, but discoloration of the abdomen is usually apparent
around the third day after death and then spreads, with gas
formation, by the end of the first week. It is delayed by freezing,
immersion or burial, and can be arrested by embalming. After
death putrefaction continues for some months. A body outdoors
in the summer may be reduced to a skeleton within weeks, but
in winter may remain largely intact until the next spring; in
most cases a body outdoors becomes a skeleton within a year.
When only bones are left, their dating is difficult and it is usually
possible to say only that death occurred more or less than fifty
to one hundred years before discovery.

The Post-Mortem

The first post-mortem examination or autopsy ('seeing with one's
own eyes') may have been performed in Byzantium around AD
800 to discover the cause of plague. There is a better-authenti-
cated report from Parma in 1286. These early examinations had
to be carried out very soon after death in the absence of any
antisepsis or refrigeration.

In many cases the cause of death remains a matter for speculation until the autopsy; the medical attendant may be in error
even when he is familiar with the patient, and doctors themselves
are the keenest advocates of autopsy when any doubt about the
diagnosis exists. But, unless it has been ordered by the coroner,
it is usually necessary to obtain permission from the relatives
before the examination can be carried out. This is obviously a
sensitive field, especially in countries such as the USA where
great importance is attached to burying an intact dead body.
Nevertheless, there are circumstances in which the public interest
must override private sorrow, as when it is necessary to exclude

an illness likely to become epidemic, or to verify that death is due to an industrial disease.

The mortuary, therefore, is an essential department of a hospital. It is often lightly referred to by the medical staff as the temple of truth, or the department of diagnostic humiliation. Bodies are brought from the wards on enclosed trolleys, each shrouded and covered with a sheet, a tag at the wrist or ankle carrying the personal details. These are entered in the post-mortem register. In most cases post-mortems are performed at a set time and if this is likely to exceed a few hours, bodies are stored in a cold room. Whether or not a post-mortem examination is made, most bodies are removed by funeral directors within a few days; but the bodies of unidentified persons – such as those of tramps who have collapsed in public places – may be held in refrigeration much longer before burial at the public expense.

The post-mortem room itself contains one or more porcelain-topped tables grooved in herring-bone fashion to allow drainage of blood and fluids. A water-hose hangs over each and there is often a wooden working surface at one end to allow removed organs to be spread out and dissected. The implements include knives, saws, a hammer and chisel, perhaps an electric saw for opening the skull and, incongruously, a domestic ladle for scooping blood from the body cavities. There is a wall-blackboard for marking the weight of each organ as it is removed : brain, heart, lungs, liver, spleen and kidneys. There are jars filled with preserving fluid to hold specimens for examination and microscopy at leisure and for demonstration to the medical staff. Many of these eventually form part of the collection in the hospital's pathological museum.

The department is run by the mortuary technician, often a highly experienced man who may begin the examination pending the arrival of the pathologist. On each side an incision is made extending from the angle of the jaw to the upper end of the breastbone in the midline, forming a V; and from the angle so formed a long incision is made right down the length of the body in the midline. The rib cartilages are cut through on each side so that the front of the chest-wall can be lifted away to expose the heart and lungs. The tongue, larynx, heart and lungs are removed *en bloc,* then the abdominal organs. Each organ is washed under the hose, inspected externally, then sliced serially on the wooden surface. Another incision is made across the vault of the skull from ear to ear, flaps of scalp are turned forward and backward to expose the cranium, and the skull-cap is removed using a hand-saw or an electric saw so that the brain may be lifted out.

When the examination is complete, the organs are returned to the body or otherwise disposed of, the incisions are sewn up by the technician, and the body cleaned and tidied for the funeral director. Relatives often desire to see the body after the post-mortem, so it is made as presentable as possible.

Death and the Dissecting Room

A regular supply of bodies is required by the nation's medical schools for their students to dissect. In the past it has been an essential part of preclinical training to dissect the entire body over a period of some eighteen months. In recent years, however, the anatomy requirements have become less stringent for the ordinary undergraduate and there has been less actual dissection and more teaching from preparations and models.

Bodies for the dissecting room were not, in the past, always easy to come by. Dissection is not known to have begun in England until the end of the fifteenth century, though some demonstrations on the corpses of criminals were authorized in the reign of Henry VIII. During the nineteenth century only the bodies of hanged criminals were available – in fact, their dissection was compulsory by law. But this source proving inadequate, the snatching of freshly-buried corpses by 'resurrection men' became prevalent, a lucrative trade for the ruffians concerned. Increasing public anger was aroused, especially when murders were committed specifically to obtain bodies for sale. The disclosures at the Edinburgh trial of the infamous Burke and Hare in 1828 were ultimately responsible for the Anatomy Act of 1831, which regularized the conduct of anatomy schools and authorized the use of unclaimed bodies for dissection.

The Act established the office of Inspector of Anatomy. At one time there were several Inspectors; now there is one for the whole country who supervises and licenses schools and teachers of anatomy and operative surgery and regulates the provision of 'subjects'. Traditionally, such subjects have come from two main sources. There are the unclaimed bodies of those who die in hospitals, asylums and reception centres. There are also the better-nourished bodies of the enlightened middle-class who have bequeathed them in life for medical research.

Those who wish so to bequeath their bodies can do so by writing to the Professor of Anatomy at a recognized medical school, or to the Inspector of Anatomy at the Department of Health. They do not sign a form; this is the task of their executors or next-of-kin, who should inform the school or the Inspector as soon as possible after the death of the donor. If the body is accepted a funeral director will be sent to remove it. It is not always accepted for it may have been recently operated on or been the subject of a post-mortem; it may require investigation by a coroner, or may be from a populous area with an already adequate supply of bodies. A body used for dissection must be buried or cremated within two years. Some medical schools allow the next-of-kin to arrange a private funeral or pay for a simple ceremony themselves; others insist that after the body has been handed over, there shall be no further contact between the school and the executors.

Cryonics

During the last fifteen years some Americans have tried to solve the problem of mortality by freezing bodies immediately after death, with the object of reviving them at some future date when the diseases that killed them will have become curable.

This is a case of an untenable theory based on some genuine medical and biological observations. It has long been known that individuals frozen in the snow, and apparently dead, can recover from their hypothermic state if they are rewarmed. Organs, cells and tissues can be kept deep-frozen for months and years and then reanimated. Japanese scientists perfused a cat's brain with glycerol – which prevents disruptive crystallization during freezing – and stored it at $-20°C$ for 203 days; on rewarming there was normal electroencephalographic activity, indicating that even nerve cells can survive and be revived after long-term refrigeration. The frozen storage of the sperm and ova of livestock is now routine. In 1972, workers of the US Atomic Energy Commission stored embryos taken from the wombs of pregnant mice for eight days at the temperature of liquid nitrogen; after thawing they were transferred to the wombs of foster mice, where they resumed normal development. Small animals, even small mammals, have been frozen and successfully revived.

In January 1967, James Bedford, a retired professor of psychology in California, had himself deep-frozen after his death from cancer. His body was perfused with chemicals, packed in dry ice and, later, placed in a capsule of liquid nitrogen near absolute zero, in Phoenix, Arizona. There he remains, frozen, waiting for a cure for cancer to be found.

Cryonic (from the Greek *kryos*: icy cold) societies sprang up all over the United States. Within two years nine other people had followed his grisly example. The body, as soon as possible after death, is placed in ice packs; it has its blood drawn off through the jugular vein and a saline solution pumped in. It is then put into an insulated box packed with dry ice and, via a temporary coffin lined with zinc, eventually rests in a huge blue and white cylinder resembling a bathroom boiler in appearance. The cost is about £6,000, with another £9,000 to provide the necessary income for maintenance.

Unfortunately, despite the apparently encouraging results with small animals, medical opinion is firmly against the process. If the pseudoscience of cryonics, designed for human storage and revival, were to have any chance of success, it would have to be carried out *before* death, and the relevant ethical and technical problems would be mind-boggling. Medical critics have pointed out that a corpse kept at the recommended temperature of $-190°C$ suffers irreversible changes and that the freezing process itself is cell-damaging, also that it is not possible to freeze and rewarm a human body as uniformly as that of a small animal.

Such criticisms have not daunted the promoters of cryonics. One said: 'That is just the sort of thing they said to Galileo'. The promoters, as might be expected, have appeared in large numbers since the idea of deep-freezing human beings has become more popular. Leaflets are distributed with the potent message: 'Freeze. Wait. Reanimate'. A rash of firms with names like Continue-Life Corporation, Juno Inc. and the Life Extension Society have appeared in the United States, and interest has spread to Britain. The Life Extension Society now has branches in Britain, co-ordinated by a postal worker from Swansea.

> For I must die,
> There is no remedy.
>
> GEORGE BOLEYN,
> Viscount Rochford

The Major Causes of Death

Until fairly recent times, the major causes of death throughout the world were infections – particularly tuberculosis, smallpox, poliomyelitis and parasitic diseases – starvation, malignant disease and violent death; and natural death in old age often tended to be distinctly rare. This is still the case in the more backward parts of the globe. But in the more affluent countries of the West things have changed. Fatal infections have been virtually abolished; we have forgotten how tuberculosis and infantile paralysis used to scourge us. Apart from war, violent deaths have diminished, though it must be remembered that traffic accidents take a continuous toll and are, indeed, the major cause of death among young men. Malignant disease is still with us, and there is a rising incidence of cancer of the lung, perhaps also of the breast, bowel and uterus.

What is *new* in Europe and America is that the commonest cause of death in middle and later life is now disease of the heart and blood vessels. This constitutes a virtual epidemic, which is affecting younger and younger age groups and spreading to women as well as men; it is the major cause of death in the United Kingdom. It is due to the arterial disease of atherosclerosis, in which there occur calcified plaques containing cholesterol deposits in the vessel walls. This involves the coronary arteries of the heart, giving rise to coronary heart disease or ischaemic heart disease. Clinically, this is manifested as coronary thrombosis (myocardial infarction, heart-attack), angina of effort, or sudden death.

Many types of clinical and epidemiological study are currently being carried out into this group of disorders. To summarize the results of these investigations so far, the following points may be made. There is a genetic aspect: premature death from ischaemic heart disease tends to run in families; so does longevity with relative immunity from coronary disease. There is also a hereditary condition of hypercholesteraemia, in which the blood contains abnormally high levels of cholesterol from an early age, so predisposing to early arterial disease. The disorder is much commoner in men; this may be for hormonal reasons, or because men are often more sedentary than women and more exposed to occupational stress, or because they are heavier smokers, for smoking is known to excite coronary spasm. (But now that more women are going out to work and smoking heavily, they too show an increasing incidence of cardiovascular disease.) Obesity, diabetes and high blood-pressure are strongly correlated with coronary disease. Regular vigorous physical exercise seems to be a safeguard. The death-rate also appears to have some relation to the degree of hardness of the water-supply. The most vexed question of all is whether there is a link with a diet containing a high proportion of saturated animal fats including cholesterol. This is still very much under debate; but the general trend of medical opinion is in favour of such a view and current medical advice is to eschew butter, milk, eggs and fatty meats in favour of margarine or other spreads containing unsaturated fats, vege-table oils for salads and cooking, and fish. Studies have been made which purport to show that such a diet reduces the inci-dence of primary heart disease and increases the survival time in those who have already suffered heart-attacks. But it is fair to point out that there is a minority opinion which pins the blame on sugar and refined starches rather than making choles-terol the villain of the piece.

It is impossible to summarize here all the current research

into the prevention and control of cancer. Epidemiological study constitutes one such approach. This deals with the differential incidence of cancer in different races and communities, and the elucidation of factors that seem to be causal or precipitant : smoking in lung cancer, certain industrial chemicals in cancer of the bladder, etc. Another approach is the immunological one. This is based on the idea that cancer cells develop from time to time within the normal body and are continuously destroyed by the body's 'immunological surveillance system', and that it is the failure of this system with ageing that eventually permits clinical cancer to develop. If the natural defences can be encouraged, if protective anti-tumour sera developed by injecting tumour cells into animals are used in treatment, the outlook may be greatly changed for the better. Susceptible populations can be screened in order to facilitate early detection of the disease, e.g. cancer of the breast or cervix can be routinely looked for in apparently healthy women of the appropriate age groups on a regional or even a national scale. Biochemical and other tests are in the process of elaboration which indicate the existence of a cancer that is still clinically undetectable. The classical forms of treatment of established malignant disease are being continually improved to provide better forms of therapy with irradiation, cytotoxic and steroid agents. And if it is proved that viruses are important in causing cancer, the possibility may arise of prevention by means of vaccines.

Organ and Tissue Transplants

It is certain that the range and success-rate of the grafting of organs and tissues from the body of a live or dead donor into a recipient patient will increase as the years pass. The main problems in such grafting are the speediest possible transfer of the graft in as healthy a condition as possible; the maintenance of the grafted organ in good condition in its new owner; and the ethical considerations that arise.

This is a controversial subject with medical, legal, ethical and even religious aspects. These are less onerous in the case of *living* donors of organs, usually kidneys; such donors must have a full written explanation of the procedure and sign a witnessed form of consent, and the donation must not hazard the life or health of the donor. For the donation of *cadaver* tissues or organs there must have been previous consent during life, and in its absence organs should not be taken without the written consent of the nearest relatives, or unless it was known that there was no objection during life. If there are no traceable relatives, and in cases not reported to the coroner, the charge of bodies under existing legislation is usually vested in the hospital management committee and the committee may permit an autopsy for removal of organs.

Ethically, it is unacceptable to transfer an ill or dying person to another hospital so as to be nearer a potential recipient. It is not permissible to carry out tissue-typing or other studies on a dying patient if these are in the recipient's rather than the donor's interests. Yet, because of the need for urgent removal of organs after death – since they deteriorate so rapidly after loss of their blood-supply – some dying patients are inevitably regarded as prospective donors and any prospective recipient must be prepared in advance of the donor's death. Hence the importance of determining the precise moment of death, and we have noted that it is fallacious to suppose that cessation of breathing and heartbeat are necessarily identical with bodily death. Clinical judgement must be supplemented by a number of diagnostic aids, of which electroencephalography is currently the most helpful. Death must be pronounced in transplant cases by two fully-registered practitioners, at least one of whom must be five-years qualified, who are totally independent of the team undertaking the transplant. A particularly poignant problem is that of deciding whether or when to switch off the respirator which is maintaining a vegetable existence in patients whose brain activity has been abolished by head injury and who never

regain consciousness. Here too, the decision must not be influ-
enced by organ transplant requirements. Finally, the anonymity
of donor and recipient should be respected; this is sometimes
difficult when news of heart transplants hits the headlines.

Less well known are the purely medical problems of infection
and rejection by the host tissues after transfer. Infection usually
responds to antibiotics, but rejection is due to a natural immune
response to what the recipient body regards as foreign matter,
and this process tends to build up with the passage of time. It
can be modified or reduced in various ways : by administering
drugs that suppress the immune reaction (but which lessen resistance to infection), by giving a serum that combats the defending
lymphocytes of the blood, or by irradiating the host. However,
the problem of rejection is not yet altogether solved, and rejection is the cause of eventual failure in many cases where organ
transplants have gone well for a few years. It is of interest that
tissues which have no blood-supply of their own, such as the
cornea of the eye, do not excite this response, so that anyone
can donate a cornea to anyone else. In the case of blood-transfu-
sion, which is only a special form of tissue transplant, the risk
is not so much of ultimate rejection as of immediate incompati-
bility, with clumping of the donor's cells and resulting circulatory
disasters. This was eliminated once it was recognized that any
individual belongs to one of a small number of blood-groups in
which definite rules govern intercompatibility. More recently,
essentially similar principles have been applied to tissue-typing
donor and recipient to establish the conditions most favourable
for organ transfer.

The organ most commonly grafted is the kidney, and the
success-rate for grafting a kidney from a living near-relative is
high. This is partly because of good tissue compatibility; partly
because this is a planned procedure in which removal and im-
plantation of the kidney can be done in the same operating
theatre without any delay. The success-rate for transplantation
of cadaver kidneys falls off sharply in comparison, and any graft,

however successful initially, may eventually be lost by rejection except when the donor kidney has come from a live twin. Because of the importance of immunological considerations to long-term kidney transplant survival, it is now routine to tissue-type all potential recipients (in practice this means those sufferers from chronic nephritis whose life-expectancy is threatened and who, very often, survive only thanks to regular dialysis on an artificial kidney at home or in hospital).

The problem of saving these sufferers is an agonizing one. There are not enough machines to keep them all alive. Some 7,000 persons die of renal failure every year, and perhaps 2,000 of these would have lived if a kidney machine had been available. Now, once a machine is in regular use for a specified patient it is not available for anyone else, at those times in the week, until that patient either dies or successfully receives a kidney transplant. Further, it costs several thousand pounds a year to maintain a patient on a machine.

All this underlines the importance of increasing the supply of donor kidneys from its present inadequate level. This can be achieved, to some extent, by increasing the efficiency of the transplant services. In 1972 the Department of Health set up a national organ-matching service in Bristol, where the names of patients waiting for kidneys are kept on a computer. When donor kidneys become available, information is flashed to this centre and the most suitable recipient is chosen on the basis of tissue-typing and geographical location. The Bristol centre is linked with the Euro-transplant service at Leiden, in Holland, which keeps a similar computerized list, so that a kidney donation service is effective throughout Europe, the organs being transported by air.

However, such co-operation within the medical profession is not enough to keep up with the demand. Even doctors are not always sufficiently aware of the possibilities when dealing with cases of sudden death; the victims of traffic accidents or heart attacks are often eminently suitable donors, but many casualty officers fail to recognize this and nurses are not always well-disposed to the procedure. Taking into account the fear of a hostile reaction from the relatives and the need to remove organs speedily after death, it is not surprising that little use is made of this large potential source.

An alternative approach is for potential donors to express consent during life, and in 1972 the Department of Health began issuing donor cards on which anyone can indicate that his kidneys may be used after his death, the intention being to create a climate of opinion favouring permission for kidney transplantation. These cards must be carried at all times and it is essential for a donor to discuss the matter with his family in advance, for many relatives otherwise refuse permission while still in a state of shock, or consent only after a delay which imperils or negates a successful transfer. But the idea is spreading, and one London hospital reports that the proportion of refusals from relatives of the dying fell from a half in 1972 to a fifth more recently. We may note that in Scandinavia doctors are empowered to remove any organ after death.

Ethical considerations of an entirely different nature also apply to organ transplants. These reflect the possible danger of ours becoming an over-compassionate society, in which an increasing number of sick and diseased people are kept alive by a decreasing number of healthy working people. It can be maintained that transplantation is an anti-evolutionary procedure which militates against the normal wastage of unhealthy stock and encourages the survival of the unfit. The proposition is highly debatable.

Organs other than the kidney are transplanted far less frequently. Liver transplantation presents formidable technical difficulties, though the risk of rejection is smaller. Many hospitals maintain a 'bone-bank' in which segments of bone are stored in preservatives or after irradiation for grafting in orthopaedic operations. Here there is no controversy; bones seem to be less emotive than internal organs and they are *dead* grafts which can be removed at quite a late stage after death.

The most emotive transplant, of course, is that of the heart. Up to June 1973 213 heart transplants had been performed since Professor Barnard's epoch-making operation and thirty-four of these patients were still alive. There is currently a lull in the use of this procedure in most centres; the problem of late rejection and the cost and concentration of equipment and skilled personnel required constitute formidable obstacles to heart transplantation becoming a routine procedure. It is at least as likely that equally successful results will eventually follow the introduction of some form of mechanical pump.

Corneal grafting to cure some forms of blindness is still hampered by a shortage of donor eyes, and there is a waiting list for the operation. The old Anatomy Act prevented surgeons from removing donor eyes in time for them to be of any use. The Corneal Grafting Act of 1952, however, allowed eyes to be collected immediately after death, and the first of many subsequent eye-banks was established at East Grinstead's Queen Victoria Hospital. The present rate of successful operations in Britain is some 170 a year. Because donor eyes must be removed without delay after death, consent in life is essential and a register of donors is kept by the Royal National Institute for the Blind.

Looking into the future, it is probable that the difficulties of rejection will eventually be overcome, and that it will be possible to store 'banks' of organs of all kinds. Technical problems, however, make it certain that it will never be possible to perform a brain transplant, for such a graft could not be connected to the recipient's spinal cord and it would be difficult to maintain its circulation. What *can* be done, though – and this is so bizarre as to be repugnant – is to transfer a whole head from one animal to another. Heads have been exchanged and an animal has been grafted with a second head. One can hardly imagine this technique being applied to man; and, philosophically, this procedure is strictly speaking to be regarded as the transplant of a body rather than a brain.

Pain

The search for relief from pain is an ancient one. 'Divine is the work to subdue pain,' wrote Hippocrates in the fourth century BC. We must distinguish between *analgesia,* the relief of pain in the conscious patient by drugs or other means, and *anaesthesia,* the abolition of all forms of sensation, usually but not always associated with loss of consciousness. Analgesia has a long history; anaesthesia is modern, unless we allow that God Himself was the first anaesthetist when He put Adam into a deep sleep for the operation of rib-removal.

The drugs used to relieve pain in past ages included alcohol and opium, mandragora and henbane. Sometimes these were used to dull the pains of execution, and the stupefied victims might then need to be given the *coup-de-grâce,* such as was, perhaps, the spear wound in the side of Christ. Homer mentions opium as a drug conferring freedom from grief and pain, and laudanum, an opium tincture, was widely used in self-medication during the nineteenth century – one thinks of Coleridge, De Quincey and other addicts.

In the past an important aspect of pain was in relation to surgical procedures. The fortitude required to undergo these operations while still conscious is almost unimaginable now. But it must be remembered that there was no alternative; it was taken for granted, people were less sensitive and more stoical, and there was less of the morbid apprehension that so enhances pain in modern times. Further, operations before anaesthesia were conducted with incredible rapidity, an amputation through the thigh in less than a minute. Of course, pre-operative drugs of all kinds were given; Indian surgeons would reduce the patient to a state of semi-sensibility by repeated blows along the spine before reducing a dislocation; in America a strong black cigar was sometimes inserted into the rectum.

The history of anaesthesia, from Humphry Davy's nitrous oxide to ether and chloroform, is well-known. What is not so

well-known is that, had it not been for the introduction of these
agents, hypnosis to induce insensitivity to pain might have become a respectable discipline in the nineteenth century. But while
it was on tentative trial at University College Hospital in London,
the first amputation under ether in Britain was performed there
with complete success, the surgeon remarking: 'Gentlemen, this
Yankee dodge beats mesmerism hollow!'

Many doctors and theologians continued for a time to regard
pain and suffering as a virtue, or at any rate a biological neces-
sity, especially the pains of childbirth, until opposition was stilled
by the obstetric use of chloroform for Queen Victoria herself. As
the century advanced, techniques of local and spinal anaesthesia
were also developed. In our own times we have seen the Russian
use of electrical anaesthesia, the resurgence of the ancient
Chinese technique of acupuncture, and the re-entry of hypnotism
by the back door, especially for dental extraction.

Some pain is essential as a warning to preserve the safety of
the individual. Those rare children who are congenitally insensitive to pain suffer repeated fractures because they lack this protective mechanism. When pain is abolished by such diseases of
the nervous system as leprosy and neurosyphilis, grave lesions may
result. Fortunately, most pain is temporary. Its management
becomes really pressing when it is persistent and poorly respon-
sive to drugs, as in facial neuralgia, and particularly when it is
due to incurable malignant disease, i.e. in the (often very prolonged) terminal care of the dying. Considerable progress has
been made in achieving control other than by the use of increasing doses of morphine or other addictive drugs. Some persistent
pains can be treated by the injection of alcohol or phenol into
related nerve-centres or into the spinal canal. But when pain is
unbearable, and the patient is known to be incurable, it is
possible to divide the fibre tract in the spinal cord that conveys
pain messages to the brain – the operation of spinothalamic
tractotomy.

A recent refinement of this procedure is based on the 'gate' theory that the nerve tracts for pain are capable of carrying only a limited volume of traffic, and that if these pathways are occupied by a controlled artificial stimulation, there will be no room for painful stimuli. Electrodes are implanted in or near the spinal cord and electrical stimulation, which may be given by the patient himself, will blot out the pain when it becomes intense.

A related aspect is that it is, to a large extent, fearful apprehension and preoccupation with symptoms that enhance the perception of pain. Pain is always worse when there is nothing else to think of, as at night, or when it is magnified by neurosis or psychosis, or when persons become sensitized and dread its recurrence. This aspect may be dealt with by the operation of leucotomy on the brain itself; pain is still felt, but as a kind of sensation freed of its fearful psychic component. Somewhat different procedures attack the very headquarters of pain reception in the thalamus and related areas of the brain.

The appreciation of pain is greatly affected by mood: a severe injury may be entirely unnoticed by a soldier in the heat of battle or a footballer during the game, whereas depression and lack of occupation enhance pain. This has a particular application to the care of the dying, and in this field the work of Dr Cicely Saunders at St Christopher's Hospice in London has established certain principles that have attracted worldwide attention. One is that the pain must never be allowed to dominate consciousness. Drugs must be given so regularly and frequently that it is never allowed to return, so relieving the exacerbation due to nervous apprehension. The patient can relax and think of other things. Pain *separates* a man from those around him, who feel inadequate and unable to communicate; effective pain relief can reunite a sufferer's family during his last weeks.

But much can be done without resorting to drugs. Dr Saunders has stressed that 'the doctor must sit and listen to the various facets of distress so that he may see whenever something specific or helpful can be introduced'. This 'listening' to patients is regarded as so important at the Hospice that the staff/patient ratio is kept at a high level. 'We can give a great deal of treatment, often unexpected remission or even cure, but always we hope, something of real comfort.' A splendid objective, reminiscent of the aims of the French mediaeval surgeon: *'Guérir parfois, soulager souvent, consoler toujours.'*

There is a great deal of diversional and occupational therapy at the Hospice, all made more possible by the control of pain and itself contributing to the control of pain. Because most of the patients are local, there is close contact between the Hospice and the community and the entire family becomes the unit of care. In the world of European medicine these concepts are a fairly recent innovation, the importance of which is being increasingly recognized. (See Chapter 8 for further discussion of St Christopher's Hospice and the care of the dying.)

Euthanasia

Euthanasia is the 'good' (*eu*) or 'easy' death (*thanatos*) of the Greeks, who believed that a man was entitled to a painless, comfortable end. 'If I can choose between a death of torture and one that is simple and easy, why should I not select the latter?' wrote Seneca. 'If I know that I must suffer without hope of relief I will depart not through fear of the pain itself but because it prevents all for which I would live.' This is a view that has been shared by many throughout history. Sir Thomas More urged that the anguished sufferer from an incurable disease should either dispatch himself 'or else suffer himself willingly to be rid out of life by others'. Nevertheless, while suicide is no longer a crime in this country, encouraging or aiding a person to kill himself may be punishable and carries a penalty of fourteen years' imprisonment, while 'mercy killing' remains under our present laws an act of deliberate murder, though judges often show a good deal of compassion when the circumstances are particularly harrowing.

In a modern society euthanasia is an issue of primary concern to the field of medical ethics: in almost all cases it will be a doctor who will be called upon to commit an act of euthanasia. However, it is also an issue that concerns every human being, for we are all mortal and there is always the chance that we may find ourselves in a situation where euthanasia ceases to become an abstract issue, and becomes instead our most urgent consideration.

The proponents and opponents of euthanasia agree on very little – even the definition of the term itself is in contention – and there is not the space here to treat the subject fully. However, I propose to give a brief summary of the arguments on either side and suggest books that develop them further and expound them in more detail, so that the reader may make up his own mind, for this is an argument that each man must decide for himself; indeed proponents of euthanasia would argue-that this *is* the issue: Don't we have the right to decide for ourselves?

First let us try to define the problem. Due to the advances made in medical science, more people are now living longer. Doctors can keep patients alive who a century ago would have had no chance of survival. But does this mean that doctors must, in all circumstances, contrive to keep alive those whose natural will to live has already expired? Must doctors *always* extend life when they are technically able to do so, heedless of the quality of the existence they are preserving?

David Le Vay, who contributed most of the material on the medical aspects of death in this and the preceding chapter, has written, clearly and succinctly, his views on euthanasia. He speaks for most, but certainly not all, doctors. 'It is essential to understand clearly what euthanasia is, and what it is not,' he writes. 'Euthanasia, as commonly understood, implies the definite commission of an action directly resulting in death; it is a deliberate and planned procedure. But it is possible to bring about death in another way: by acts of omission, by neglecting to take steps which could reasonably be expected to save or prolong life.' He calls this 'negative euthanasia', but sees it as 'very different from deciding to do something intended to kill'.

Mr Le Vay then goes on to specify some of the cases in which it may be felt that it is better for the individual to die than to go on living: those with severe and uncontrollable pain, due to progressive and incurable disease; the senile demented; those with severe brain damage or 'brain death' whose continuation in a living but comatose vegetable state is entirely dependent on a mechanical respirator; the newly-born child with severe deformities; and very old people with severe injuries such as multiple fractures.

'In many of these cases,' he says, 'it is possible to bring about death by simply abandoning or not instituting medical and nursing efforts. Everyone knows that this has always taken place to some extent, quietly and informally, both in homes and in hospitals. A few words may pass between doctor and nurse, nothing is written down, often nothing at all is said. The doctor simply does not prescribe the drug, the brain-damaged patient is not fed through a stomach-tube, the hideously deformed child is left untended. None of this is formalized; there is no protocol; the relatives are sometimes, but not always, allowed to understand what is happening.' He also cites another group of patients, those with advanced painful malignant disease, who 'have their dying accelerated, not by any single act, but by gradually increasing the size and frequency of the doses of pain-killing drugs'.

At this point Mr Le Vay stresses that 'nothing so far described is equivalent to positive euthanasia as envisaged by such bodies as the Euthanasia Society. "Positive euthanasia" implies a deliberate single act of homicide, to be performed by a physician or physicians under the law, at the request of the patient if he is conscious and of sound mind or that of the relatives, possibly under the *aegis* of a group of medical advisers or a medical referee. This,' he says, 'is, to put it plainly, murder as the law stands, and it is proposed that this act should be legalized and delegated to the medical profession to carry out.'

He recognizes that the advocates of voluntary euthanasia are not irresponsible and appreciate the need for stringent safeguards to ensure that the motives of all concerned are unblemished and that the decision is being made on behalf of the sufferer and not on behalf of society. But, he objects, 'it involves doctors very closely indeed. A doctor's aim is to save and prolong life; euthanasia, like abortion, is the exact opposite of this. One wonders how many doctors would elect, even legally, to kill a patient even when urged to do so by the patient himself. In many areas the effects might be far-reaching; the confidence and trust reposed by elderly patients in their doctors and nurses might well be eroded. And, of course, the Catholic view is entirely opposed to euthanasia for the incurably sick, disabled or insane. One must remember too, that the option for euthanasia would need to be based on the medical diagnosis of an inevitably fatal condition. Yet in one survey 40 per cent of diagnoses were proven incorrect at post-mortem examination; so that it would be just as possible to kill a patient unnecessarily as to hang a man for a crime he did not commit. We must remember, too, that diseases fatal today may be remediable tomorrow as medical research advances.

'The matter of "consent" is also a troubled one. Persons who are depressed and alone frequently ask to be put out of their misery, but later, with their mental balance re-established, look back with incredulity to think that they could ever have made such a request.' He makes the important point that voluntary euthanasia may simply reflect a present failure to provide adequate care for the dying.

'To sum up, there is a vast difference between not "striving officiously to keep alive" and taking positive steps to end life. We all acknowledge that the former takes place; the law takes no cognizance of it unless its attention is specifically aroused. We all recognize that there is a right time to die, and indeed a general right to die, when well-meant medical interventions are meddlesome and may only make the last few hours on earth a useless and unnecessary torment. Sometimes we should just be allowed to die, with as much dignity as we can muster, without having our hearts pummelled or shocked, without transfusions or painful and humiliating surgery. Death is part of life, as necessary as sleep.

'Having said all this, one is only too well aware that there remains a central core of sufferers – alert intelligent victims of painful incurable disease whose desire to hasten their death is far from unreasonable. But to legislate for these, to ask the healer to function as part-time executioner, these matters bristle with difficulties. Possibly many doctors would see such euthanasia as the beginning of a very slippery slope and recall that Hitler's "final solution" to the Jewish problem began with "mercy killings" of the physically and mentally handicapped in Germany's own institutions and asylums. It is perhaps a paradox that "humane" killing has so far been reserved for animals. Has the time come to apply it to human beings?'

David Le Vay has presented the issues clearly, from the standpoint of the doctor. The advocates of voluntary euthanasia would probably agree and sympathize with him on many points. They might, though, have reservations about Mr Le Vay's concept of 'negative euthanasia', which is in fact a form of compulsory euthanasia – the patient himself has no say in the matter, any more than Hitler's Jews did – for the concern of the advocates of voluntary euthanasia is essentially patient-centred, rather than doctor-centred. They ask, merely, than an individual should have the right to die so far as is humanly possible in the circumstances of his own choice, and that doctors should have the right to terminate life when they are sure that this is the patient's steadfast and properly considered wish and his condition is such that euthanasia should be administered. They see this as a moral right, akin to those other rights laid down in such charters as the Universal Declaration of Human Rights. Their aim is to make it a legal right.

So far, all attempts to get legislation on euthanasia through

Parliament have failed. A Voluntary Euthanasia Bill was presented in the House of Lords in 1969 and defeated on its second
reading. But the issue is now a live one, and after the recent
reforms of the laws pertaining to abortion, homosexuality and
divorce, it is not beyond the bounds of possibility that sooner
rather than later this issue will be one on which everyone will
have to make up his mind. As we have seen, the doctor's view is
that euthanasia occurs already, quietly and informally, and he
would rather allow this state of affairs to continue, than to be
'told' by the law 'to kill'. The advocate of euthanasia's view
is that it is far better that he be told 'to kill' by the law (and
therefore by his victim) than that he should continue to take this
decision entirely by himself. The proposed form of the law introducing euthanasia is at pains to stress that no doctor would be
forced against his conscience to administer euthanasia, but it
does institute the right for the patient to find a doctor who is
willing to carry out his request if the circumstances demand it.

The text of the Voluntary Euthanasia Bill, and of the 'Form
of Declaration' to be signed by the individual wishing for the
option of euthanasia, can be found in *Euthanasia and The Right
to Death* (Peter Owen, 1969), together with argument both for
and against euthanasia. Another book, more strongly opposed
to euthanasia, is Norman St John Stevas's *The Right to Life*
(Hodder & Stoughton, 1963).

6 | DEATH AND THE LAW

> A man's dying is more the survivors'
> affair than his own.
>
> THOMAS MANN

'They have grown up piecemeal year after year,' said a Coroner when describing the bewildering maze of laws concerning inquests, burial, cremation and the disinterment of the dead. These laws range from the Anatomy Act of 1832 and the various Burial Acts, beginning in 1852, to the Human Tissues Act of 1961. 'We should perhaps start all over again and produce something less cumbersome,' he said. 'I often have to look up points in the reference books myself.'* Certainly, while we talked he referred several times to the legal tomes on his desk.

Instrumental in tracing a path through the maze, using all the power of law to ensure that we are disposed of in an orderly fashion and without the slightest hint that anything untoward has taken place, is an important group of experts. Among the more familiar are those best-known by their official titles rather than their names: the Registrars of Births and Deaths, and Her Majesty's Coroners. We shall see that their work often interacts.

Every death in Britain has to be registered with the local Registrar of Births and Deaths, and the register must be signed in his presence, by either a relative of the dead person who was

*Just before going to press (August 1975) the Government announced its acceptance in principle of a number of recommendations made in the 1971 report of the Brodrick Committee, *Death Certification and Coroners*. New legislation will be proposed to amend the procedure for certifying the cause of death; to introduce a new certification procedure for cremation; and to modernise the law on coroners' responsibilities, including abolition of the duty of a coroners' jury to name an individual as guilty of murder, manslaughter or infanticide. The information in the following chapter outlines the law as it presently stands.

71

present at the death or in attendance at the last illness; some other relative if these cannot be found; someone else who was present at the death; or the occupier of the house in which it took place. Failing these, an inmate of the house must sign, or the person causing the disposal of the body. Registration must be made within five days of the death, or written notice of it must be sent within that time.

Medical evidence of the cause of death must be given. This is usually done by the doctor who attended the deceased during the final illness. He sends a certificate of death to the Registrar, giving what to the best of his knowledge and belief is the cause of death, the last date on which he had seen the patient alive, and whether or not he has seen the body. The doctor must also give written notice of the signing of the certificate to the inform-ant of the death. He may not charge a fee for this certificate, and the registration of a death is also free. If the death is not registered within five days (or fourteen days if written notice of the death has been sent to the Registrar) any of the witnesses of the death or the informant can be ordered to register. Failure to comply involves a penalty of £10.

These regulations may seem unnecessary or over-complicated, but forms and formalities are obviously needed to ensure that a death that has occurred in suspicious circumstances does not pass unnoticed. For example, before any funeral, burial or cre-mation can take place a certificate for disposal of the body must be delivered to the clergyman by the Registrar. If the doctor who gave the cause of death has reported it to the Coroner (either because he had not attended the patient during his last illness; or had not seen him within the last fourteen days of his life; or because the death was sudden, caused by any kind of accident, or was in any way suspicious, such as through violence or neglect; or if the medical cause was unknown) the Registrar cannot register the death until the Coroner allows him to do so. A dis-posal order can also be made by the Coroner himself.

The Coroner is a doctor or lawyer who is responsible to no

one but the Crown. Apart from investigating any death which is reported to him, he also begins inquiries into the ownership of any gold or silver which has been found, to determine whether it is treasure trove and therefore belongs to the Crown. His office is an ancient one, dating from Norman times in England. He was then the king's officer who kept an eye on the sheriff of a shire or borough, recording all deaths that were sudden or 'against the course of nature'.

He has to be informed of any death that has taken place during an operation, or after an operation following an injury, or as a result of drugs, alcoholism, poisoning, industrial disease, injuries received during military service, or suicide.

Suicides, since 1824, no longer have to be ignominiously buried at a cross-roads between the hours of 9 p.m. and 12 p.m., with a stake driven through them as a precaution against vampirism. Other penalties survived for longer. Killing oneself was considered a felony until 1961, and was punishable by forfeiture of the offender's goods and chattels to the Crown and withdrawal of the right to be given a Christian burial on consecrated ground. Indeed, suicide cases still worry officialdom. Coroners try to qualify a verdict of suicide as something that happened to the victim 'while the balance of his mind was disturbed' so as to enable him to be buried in the usual way. Without the saving grace of this formula of words the funeral service is slightly different, and there might be life insurance problems, as some policies contain a clause prohibiting payment on a suicide.

Deaths can be reported to the Coroner by the police, the doctor concerned, the Registrar, or anyone who is uneasy about the apparent cause of death. Each Coroner decides for himself what action should be taken. Usually he orders a post-mortem; sometimes an inquest.

Normally the deceased's next-of-kin has to give permission before a post-mortem can be carried out, but if one is ordered by the Coroner it is rare for anyone to appeal against it. The purpose of the post-mortem is to establish with certainty the medical cause of death, in case legal proceedings depend upon it. If the death turns out to have been due to natural causes and the Coroner is satisfied that no further investigation is necessary, he informs the Registrar.

In Scotland, the medical certificate of death given by doctors is similar to that in England. But there are no Coroners. Instead, the duties carried out in England by a Coroner are the responsibility of the Procurator Fiscal, a full-time law officer under the authority of the Lord Advocate. Unlike in England, where the Coroner is independent and autonomous, the Procurator Fiscal reports certain cases to the Crown office and it is the Lord Advocate who makes the final decision as to whether a public inquiry should be held. There are certain other differences in certificates and registration in Scotland. These and other details are given in *What To Do When Someone Dies,* a booklet published by the Consumers' Association.

The Coroner to whom I spoke seemed to be particularly well qualified for his job as he was both a doctor *and* a lawyer. He described the work of Coroner like this:

'It's a job that has evolved, and it exists mainly to determine the cause of death, to allay rumours and suspicions about the death, to draw attention to the possibility of further deaths to be expected from the same cause, to advance medical knowledge and to promote the legal interests of the deceased's family, heirs and other interested parties. I get about 4,000 deaths to deal with in any one year, of which 3,500 have been natural deaths and some 500 need inquests.'

One must remember here the difference between a medical cause of death – for instance, cancer, pneumonia or heart disease – and a legal cause, which can be natural or unnatural. Did he fall or was he pushed? The Coroner has to decide.

'When people die,' the Coroner explained, 'their relatives are often very distressed, naturally, and the Coroner is there to check that the death was due to natural causes and not to a stab in the back, or an odd accident, or manslaughter. It was described to me by one of my teachers in this way : "Supposing there's a family with an old aunt who is getting senile and the family say she might be much happier if she were pushed over. Well, the Coroner is the man who exists to protect Auntie." A recent example of this is a case of mine, an Irishman who had collapsed and died in the street. During the autopsy we found that he had been drinking extremely heavily and that the cause of death was quite simply a bruised brain caused by a fractured skull. But now the Coroner has to decide, with all the evidence available, whether he just fell, or was pushed.'

A Coroner can hold an inquest on any death, but he is legally obliged to do so if he has reasonable grounds for suspecting that it was violent or unnatural, if the death took place in prison or after a car accident, or if negligence is alleged. A Coroner's court is a court of law. Witnesses are on oath. In appearance it looks like a magistrate's court. The one I saw was single and compact, with rows of wooden stalls.

'In some courts,' said the Coroner, 'proceedings start with a proclamation in which people are asked to "draw near and give your attendance". With mine it's just a case of "Rise for the Coroner". Nobody wears a gown. Counsel don't even wear robes. It's just an inquiry. There are no two sides. I will have decided which witnesses to summon, and I hear their evidence. Nobody is on trial, and no witness is obliged to answer any incriminating questions. What I am trying to establish, mainly, are the answers to these questions : Who was the dead person? When, where and how did he come by his death? and What persons, if any, are to be charged?'

No one is accused. However, the court may say who should be charged if the inquest reveals that the death was a result of murder, manslaughter or infanticide. In certain cases the Coroner must hold an inquest with a jury. When all the witnesses have been heard the Coroner sums up, and directs the jury as to the law and the possible verdicts they may bring in.

'There are certain things I can say, and there are other things

I can't say,' explained the Coroner. 'For example, I can say that there should be a pedestrian crossing at the spot where the accident occurred; but I can't say that the driver was negligent. The jury can make a comment in what is popularly known as a "rider". The verdicts I can bring in, if the court decides that death was due to a natural cause, are accident, misadventure, industrial disease, want of attention at birth, chronic alcoholism or drug abuse, aggravated by lack of care, killed himself, as a result of premature abortion, or – when the evidence doesn't fully disclose the means by which death arose – an open verdict. When the death was such that criminal proceedings must be instituted, the verdicts are either murder, manslaughter, infanticide, complicity in the deceased's suicide, or an offence against the Road Traffic Act of 1960.'

The Coroner gave some examples of inquests in which he had been involved : 'There was an accident case in which a woman had been knocked down by a car, been taken to hospital, was treated for cuts, went home, and died that night. The witnesses to the accident included the man she was walking with arm-in-arm, the driver of the car, a bus conductor, a bus driver. I also heard evidence from the policeman who was called to the scene, the ambulance driver and the doctor who had treated her. The policeman had measured the skid marks and the position of the car and checked whether its lights were all right – and had got a statement from the woman herself.

'The story that gradually built up was that the woman and the man had been drinking. They tried to cross the road, saw the car coming, dithered, changed their minds about which way to go, and then were hit by the car. The doctor said she was alert and rational, could move her legs normally and seemed to have no fractures. But she died of a fractured thigh. What had happened was that because of the stitches in her leg, at no time had she actually been asked to walk, either at the hospital or at home. She had said that she didn't want to be helped upstairs to her bedroom, but just wanted to be left on the sofa in the living-room. The pain in her thigh would have alerted every-body, but she had been drinking so much that she didn't feel pain.

'In another case a girl had been killed after her dress had caught alight from an electric fire. The makers of the dress material denied that it could burn. So we got hold of some of the stuff and set light to it in court. It burnt like anything.

'Then there was the case of the rent collector who had been found battered to death. There was one puzzling clue : a frag-ment of glass found nearby. It didn't seem to be a broken wine-glass because no other pieces were found. Nor did the victim wear glasses. But the assailant *did*, and they caught him – in Glasgow. You can imagine the work that was done by the police in checking thousands of prescriptions for glasses.'

With slight self-mockery the Coroner shrugged off these cases as being not very typical, 'Sherlock Holmes cases'. He added : 'Very rarely do we get anything in court that's unsuspected. We usually know what witnesses are going to say from reading the case beforehand.' But his praise of the painstaking work of the police was genuine. This might be the place to examine in more detail the role of the police when they become involved after a death.

A Scotland Yard spokesman (an attractive spokeswoman, in fact, but the word is somehow clumsier) told me that all new recruits were required to complete sixteen weeks' training at Hendon, followed by a period of two years 'on the beat'. I asked what the procedure was when the police were faced with an accident or a murder.

'There are many things they have to do, whether it's an industrial accident, a road traffic accident or a murder, and the order in which they do them is not always the same. In a road accident it might be that the officer has to treat an injury first, or radio for help, or clear the scene of bystanders. But he's got to do these very soon, and get statements from witnesses, make sure that an ambulance has been called and get the traffic moving. He will try to identify the victim by looking in a bag or wallet. All this he has learnt how to do during his first sixteen weeks, where he has studied basic law and practised the technique of accident investigation on a mock-up of an accident. He has, as soon as possible after the accident, measured skid marks and the distance the person was thrown. He might go with the victim in the ambulance, or he might have to break the news to the next-of-kin. (But that isn't something that's taught at Hendon. It's a horrible thing to have to do, though in the case of a fatal accident it's most likely that the victim's local police will have to do it. It's just one of the more unpleasant tasks that a police-man has, like finding a body that has been dead for months.)

'If it's a murder that the policeman has found, or something that looks like a murder, he tries to see if the victim is dead or not, then contacts his station where the CID and the police sur-geon will be informed. He touches nothing that he hasn't got to, and keeps anyone else from doing so. Several other experts arrive, such as the finger-print officer, the photographer and the Scene of Crime officer. The body is identified, or we hope so, speci-mens are taken to the laboratory, and the investigation starts. Usually a "murder room" is set up in the station nearest to where the crime took place, and there is a special suitcase which is used at the scene of the crime. Called the "murder bag", it contains all that could be needed for much of the work of gather-ing clues. Among the contents are tweezers, dusting powder, brushes, bottles for specimens, a tape measure, a ruler, a tape recorder, a magnifying glass, a torch, a mirror and a compass.'

The Coroner may open an inquest merely to establish the ident-ity of the deceased, and then adjourn it immediately so that the police can carry out further investigations. On the question of adjournments, the Coroner I spoke to emphasized that there were times when he had no option but to adjourn, whether the public liked it or not. 'I might open an inquest and then the police say that there may be a charge, so the first thing I have to do is adjourn the inquest for a month. I have to explain that I can't issue cremation certificates under these circumstances. Another example is a serious plane crash. There's obviously no point in holding an inquest before we've sorted out who is among the bodies. In fact if the victims have been badly burned it might take a year before death can be registered. If the relatives don't know this, they get very steamed up.

'When there are a lot of bodies resulting from a plane crash or a bad train crash, identification is a very complex job. Each body – or part of a body – is given a number. All the clothing is carefully collected, and sometimes we're glad to have a piece of material with the maker's name on it. Other clues are the effects, like passports and rings, and of course we hope to establish the sex of the victim and whether he's had any operations. We try to match all these elements with the details we've been given of those who were on the plane. Their dental records are sometimes vitally important as being the only possible identification.

'I remember one man identified his daughter only by the kink in her nose. But he had insisted on doing this. It is quite wrong for the public to imagine that we put all the parts of bodies in a large hangar and then invite the public to mill about, trying to identify their relatives. That is how it is done in some other countries, but not here.

'After one very bad crash we were telephoned every day from Scotland, where a man was asking if we had identified his fiancée yet. He gave us an important fact : the girl, he said, had lost the little finger of her left hand some time ago. I couldn't remember having seen a body with a finger missing on the left hand. I checked with the pathologist who was also working on the identification. He hadn't seen one with a finger off, either.

'That night I was here until late, alone, going over some of the puzzles we were trying to solve. So I went over all the hands I could find, again. There was none with the finger off; *but* there was one with a nail off the little finger of the left hand, and there was an engagement ring on the next finger. I rang up the man in Scotland and said, slowly, "Did you mean that your fiancée had lost a finger or a finger-nail?" I didn't get any further. He broke down and said it was a finger-nail he had meant.'

Unidentified bodies pose special problems. A Coroner has to take care not to authorize too readily the burial of an unknown person. If he is obliged to because there are no facilities for re-frigeration – or even a mortuary – he makes sure that any personal property or clothing is kept in case it can help towards identification later. In some parts of the country the police have photographs taken of the body. And records of dental treatment are an important help.

There are cases where it is difficult to define just what amounts to a body. The remains could be a foetus, or a limb, or a few bones and ashes. If the place where old human remains have been found (even if it is a complete skeleton) happens to be over a burial ground that has been consecrated or an ancient 'plague pit', the Coroner will probably not think an inquest is necessary. But in other cases he may, and if bones are to be removed a licence must be obtained from the Home Secretary.

In the case of mutilated bodies it is generally considered desirable to have some vital organ to justify the holding of an inquest. This is because the removal of a limb may not by itself cause death. So the Coroner who opens an inquest on an incomplete human body usually adjourns it to allow time for other parts to be found which can prove death has occurred.

With skeletons, calcined remains and ashes, the first fact to establish is whether the remains are human. Then, was the death natural or violent? If the latter, an inquest has to be held. This may be so even if the body has been totally destroyed or is irrecoverable, in which case the Coroner reports the fact to the Secretary of State, who orders the inquest.

To enable an inquest to be held on a body which has already been buried, the Coroner concerned can order its exhumation. But when an inquest has been completed, he has no power to

exhume. If the High Court decides that a new inquest is necessary, it can authorize exhumation.

It is essential that the body is seen by the Coroner either
before the inquest or during it. If he does not, the inquest is
void, unless the corpse is irrecoverable or destroyed. If the body
has been buried before the Coroner has seen it, it must be exhumed, unless he feels that it has been buried so long that it is
not going to help him with his inquest, or that there is a danger
of infection in exhuming it. In this case he does not hold the
inquest.

To disinter a body without lawful authority, whether for
dissection, or sale, or even for a purpose that is quite pious or
laudable, or even if it has been disinterred during building
operations, is a misdemeanour in common law. It is also illegal
to remove any body without the Secretary of State's licence,
except when it is being removed from one consecrated place of
burial to another. It is also illegal to expose a dead body near
a public highway where it may be seen by passers-by and in such
a way as to shock public decency.

When a death occurs on a British ship at sea, the master must
record any death on board and send the details to the Registrar
General of Shipping.

In the case of a death taking place abroad, it must be registered by the relevant Consular Officer on a certificate obtained
from the Registrar General's office in London or, if the deceased
was resident in Scotland, from the Registrar General for Scotland. A death on a foreign ship or aircraft counts as a death
abroad.

If a member of the Forces dies abroad, the Ministry of Defence
pays for his funeral there. If the family prefers, it is sometimes
possible to fly the body home. But once it has reached the undertaker in Britain it becomes the family's responsibility to pay the
funeral costs. The Ministry of Defence gives a grant of £10, or
£5 and a coffin. In some countries the Ministry can arrange
for cremation and have the ashes sent home.

In the case of a civilian dying abroad, the cost of bringing the body back can be several hundred pounds because some airlines charge twice the normal cargo rate for a body in a coffin. There may also be special requirements, such as the body being enclosed in a crate or airtight box, or that it should be embalmed.

Burying a body at sea is considered to be the same as removing it out of the country, and the Coroner must be informed. Anyone can be buried at sea at least three miles beyond the low-water mark. The master of the ship being used should know the local tides and coast well enough to ensure that the body sinks properly and permanently. If a coffin is used, it must be weighted and have holes bored in it to make sure it sinks.

When an inquest is over, the Coroner sends a certificate-after-inquest to the Registrar, which gives him the information he needs to register the death.

Usually, the person who is the informant of the death goes in person to the Registrar's office. The informant should check the draft of the proposed entry in the register to make sure there is nothing misleading in it. The Registrar himself makes the entry in the register and asks the informant to check and sign it. The informant should sign with the pen offered by the Registrar, who has to use special ink for the register.

It is important for the informant to make a note of the number of the entry in the register and the date, and of the registration district, because it is likely that several copies of the entry will be needed. The certificate which registers the death is free, but is of use only for claiming National Insurance benefits such as Death Grant and Widow's Benefit from the Department of Health and Social Security.

For claiming probate, or for private claims such as life insurance and pension schemes, a 'standard' death certificate is required, costing 50p. For claims from a registered Friendly Society, either the standard 50p certificate can be used or another which costs 15p.

But neither the standard nor the Friendly Society certificates can be used for claiming in connection with insurance taken out on the life of grandparent or parent by a child, adopted child, stepchild or grandchild. For this you need a 'special' certificate which costs 15p. Only one of these is issued to any one person. So if more than one insurance company is involved, the certificate has to be used in turn by each. If the original is lost or destroyed, a duplicate can be obtained only if the applicant makes a statutory declaration in front of a JP, magistrate, or Commissioner for Oaths.

For claims under the Family Allowances Act, National Insurance Act or National Insurance (Industrial Injuries) Act; or when probate is not required; or for cashing National Savings Certificates, Post Office or Trustee Savings Bank deposits or Premium Savings Bonds, yet another type of death certificate, costing 15p, is needed.

If you find the range of certificates confusing, take with you to the Registrar a list of the various purposes for which you think some evidence of the death might be required. If a further supply of certificates is needed later on, you can get them, but they are more expensive. For example, if the death was registered about a year before, standard death certificates can be obtained from the General Register Office at Somerset House, London. The charge is 75p if you go in person, £1.25 if you apply by post.

Special rules apply for registering a stillbirth (a stillborn child is one born after the twenty-eighth week of pregnancy which did not at any time breathe or show other signs of life. The death of a foetus before the twenty-eighth week of pregnancy is usually considered a miscarriage and does not fall within the legal definition of a stillbirth).

Registering a stillbirth has to be done within forty-two days and is a combination of registering a birth and registering a death. As for live births, the people qualified to register it comprise a list of those nearest to it, starting with the mother, and then the father – if the child would have been legitimate had it been born alive. A certificate of stillbirth is given by a doctor if he was in attendance at the time or, if not, a midwife. If neither was present, the certificate is given by one of the parents or someone who was in the house. They make a declaration on a special form, Number 35, that to the best of their knowledge and belief the child was stillborn. If there is any doubt whether the child was born alive or not, the case must be reported to the Coroner.

Once a certificate for disposal has been obtained from the Registrar or the Coroner, it is given to the undertaker or taken direct to the church, cemetery or crematorium officials. Without it they will not bury or cremate a body.

The Registrar can issue a disposal certificate before registering a death – but only when he has received the necessary information and is simply waiting for the informant to sign the register. For example, the only suitable informant could be ill in hospital but the funeral has to take place. However, such a disposal certificate authorizes burial only; crematorium officials do not accept it.

Let us endeavour so to live that when
we come to die even the undertaker
will be sorry.
MARK TWAIN

DISPOSING OF THE DEAD

In disposing of his dead, man has made an almost infinite number of variations on two basic methods: burying – whether in
the ground, in tombs, or, metaphorically, at sea – and burning.

On one small island in Melanesia the dead are disposed of in
twenty-one different ways. In other parts of the world, Muslims
are buried on their right sides, facing Mecca, while Buddhists
lie with their heads towards the north (which was Buddha's
dying position). In Japan some corpses are placed sitting upright
in tub-shaped coffins and in the past certain districts would also
observe the custom of burying the dead in one place and erecting
a tomb in another, where they would worship the spirit of the
dead. The place where the body was buried was the 'body tomb';
the other being the 'worship tomb', which was often in a temple
compound conveniently near the dead man's home. This custom
stemmed from the idea that the physical body was only a temporary home for the spirit, and, at death, could be disposed of,
whereas the spirit had to be respected and worshipped.

Bronze Age Gauls cremated their dead, as did the Etruscans
in the fourth century BC. In the Hindu Kush they buried their
dead standing up in the snow. In Assam important people are
smoke-dried before being buried two months later; in Europe
the custom of burying the dead in tombs with the four-wheeled
chariot which had acted as their hearse dated from the seventh
century AD; and Scandinavian seamen from the eighth century

85

AD were buried with a ship to carry them to the land of the dead. In Venice the hearses are gondolas, continuing the tradition of using ships as hearses and as funeral pyres, towed out to sea and left to drift. The Scythians slaughtered the dead man's wife and servants to keep him company and look after his needs. Greeks were buried with a coin in the mouth to pay the ferryman across the Styx. Throughout history, soldiers have been brought home from foreign campaigns to be buried in their homeland; thus, at the end of the Second World War, the Americans disinterred 225,000 of their war dead from Europe and Japan and reburied them in the United States.

One further method of disposal should perhaps be mentioned here, that of exposure to birds of prey, which was practised in Mexico, East Africa, Mongolia, and among the ancient Persians and Parsees.

Most societies use much more ritual than is strictly necessary to dispose of their dead. Elaborate rituals are, of course, more important to the living than the dead. They are an opportunity to underline such important concepts as faithfulness in marriage and the grief of a widow. Her wailing at the graveside can no longer help her husband, but in many parts of the world it is expected of her and is an important part of the fabric holding the society together.

Underlying all these customs is a conflict between the desire to keep alive the bond between the deceased and his sorrowing relatives, on the one hand; and on the other, the horror of death and the dead, and the fear that the deceased might return – as a ghost. This might explain the fervour of some of the rites intended to help him in the after-life. Do the members of his family want to help speed his way to paradise or are they really trying to make sure he does not return?

Most death customs are a compromise between the two points of view, and it is sometimes difficult to decide whether a rite is intended to protect the living or the dead. Careful disposal of the dead was first practised by Neanderthal man, and the custom of putting treasure, tools or implements in the grave was known in Paleolithic times. The more of his goods that were sent with the dead man, the less likely he was to return for them. To prevent the soul from 'walking' some tribes break a corpses's bones or tie the arms and knees to the chest.

The body may have to be carried out through a hole in a wall which has been specially made so that the ghost will not find its way back, and mourners in dusty countries sometimes even rub out their footprints. But in other places familiarity with the corpse is the custom; mourners have been known to lie down on it, kiss it, anoint themselves with the exuding fluid or even, as in north-eastern Siberia, play cards on it. As late as the nineteenth century, in Lincolnshire, a dead man's feet were tied together to prevent him from returning. In other parts of Britain there was a superstition that as murdered people were particularly likely to become restless wanderers after death, their footwear should be removed. In 1889 a policeman in the Isle of Arran in Scotland hid a murder victim's shoes.

Funerals have varied from the cremation of gypsy kings and queens by setting their caravans alight, to the opulent bad taste surrounding the burials of film stars and hoodlums in the 1930s, and the dancing, jazz-playing and singing that used to be characteristic of funerals in New Orleans.

However, the basis of most customs has been religious belief. Buddhists believe that death is not an end but the beginning of a new existence for an enlightened person. It is thus important to meditate upon death. Proper preparation for death is essential, because one's last thoughts determine the way one will be reborn. To Jews, being properly lamented over can be almost as important as being correctly buried. In Islam, the funeral procession is always followed on foot, because that is how the angels of God go. Before the tomb is closed, two tutors speak urgently into the dead man's ears. They are prompting him on the correct answers he must give when he is being catechized by the angels on such questions as 'Who is your God?' and 'Who is your Prophet?' During the long and complicated ceremonies which are essential for a Hindu, the dying person must if possible touch a cow, which is then handed over to a priest. Another Hindu belief is that only a son can properly perform the funeral rites which will ensure his father's rebirth into a new and happy life. Hence the desire for male children.

Cemeteries

In pagan times, burial places were considered sacred and were located outside the centres of population. Indeed, before the advent of Christianity, it was actually against the law to bring the dead into a city.

This practice was carried on by the early Christians. Their cemeteries – the word derives from the Greek *koimeterion,* meaning a sleeping place or dormitory – were generally outside the city walls and were independent of the Church. However, inspired perhaps by the Catacombs in Rome, the custom of burying the dead in tombs in or under the churches themselves gradually emerged. It was at this point that the problem, which was to confront the authorities in charge of burying the dead for centuries, emerged for the first time : the problem of space. Within a short time the churches were filled with corpses, and an alternative burying-place had to be found.

In 752 St Cuthbert obtained papal permission to add church-yards to churches. These were areas of land, immediately sur-rounding the churches, which could be enclosed, consecrated and used for burials. From this point, only the rich or famous were able to take their rest inside the church; everyone else was buried outside in the churchyard.

For nearly a thousand years the system worked well in Britain, but the population had meanwhile expanded rapidly and with it the towns and cities. By Stuart times the urban churchyards were grossly overcrowded. John Evelyn, in his *Diary,* describes them as 'filled up with earth, or rather the congestion of dead bodies one above the other, to the very top of the walls, and some above the walls. . . .' Frequent outbreaks of plague added considerably to the problem and finally forced the authorities to think seriously about finding a new way of disposing of the dead, or at least new places in which to bury them. Evelyn and his contemporary Sir Christopher Wren were among those who proposed the building of cemeteries, but they were ignored, partly because of religious bigotry.

For 200 more years the situation continued to deteriorate; burial services became increasingly careless and burial grounds impossibly overcrowded. Coffins were laid one on top of another until they were just below the surface, while sextons surreptitiously made room for more by removing bones and partly decayed remains. In the nineteenth century tons of bones were sent every year from London to northern cities to be crushed in special mills and sold as fertilizer. In 1880 it was reported that soil from the Whitfield Tabernacle was being sold to florists in Camden Town. Body-snatchers were making the most of the situation, and grave-diggers were removing coffin-handles and nails for selling. The stench of the polluted air understandably drove many grave-diggers and 'mutes' (hired funeral attendants) to almost permanent drunkenness on rum, and many are said to have died from the concentration of gases and corruption.

At last the conscience of the nation was aroused and the concept of cemeteries finally found favour with the authorities. Huge commercial undertakings like the General Cemetery Company, founded in 1830, were formed to meet the growing demand for cemeteries where people could pay their respects to the dead in suitable, sanitary surroundings. Among several sites seriously considered for a graveyard was Primrose Hill, to the north of Regent's Park. But in 1831 the company bought fifty-four acres in what was then open countryside at Kensal Green. The following year this site, bought for £9,400, became the first of Britain's great metropolitan cemeteries.

The site was divided, writes J. S. Curl in *The Victorian Cele-*

bration of Death, by the Regent's Canal. The thirty-nine acres
to the north of the canal were consecrated by the Bishop of
London, but not the fifteen acres to the south of it, which were
reserved for Dissenters. Another insight into the clergy of the day
was the arrangements made to compensate those whose salaries
had been made up largely of burial fees. For example, the Rector
of St Marylebone received half-a-crown for each body from his
parish that was buried at Kensal Green. In addition, compensation of five shillings was received by any clergyman in London
whose former parishioners were buried in a vault or a brick grave
at the new cemetery. If the grave was in the open ground, the
compensation was only one shilling and sixpence.

By 1839 Kensal Green was a flourishing concern. The value
of the company's original £25 shares had more than doubled.
Burial charges ranged from 25 shillings for a simple grave to 15
guineas for a vault or a grave made of brick. The cemetery
became one of the sights of London. Among those buried there
are the writers Trollope, Thackeray and Browning; the artists
Millais, Leigh Hunt and Cruickshank; and Brunel, the engineer.

Another famous private cemetery, best-known now perhaps as
the last resting place of Karl Marx, was opened in Highgate in
1839. Its fifty acres had been purchased by the London Cemetery
Company three years earlier. By 1888 it contained 25,000 graves.
Among them are those of George Eliot, Michael Faraday, and
Elizabeth Siddall. She was the wife of Dante Gabriel Rossetti, the
painter and poet. Seven years after she was buried a bizarre
incident took place that reflected the macabre romanticism of
the age. In life she had been renowned for the brilliance of
her hair, which was long and of a reddish gold. Before her
coffin had been closed, her grieving husband had placed the
manuscript of his poems beside her. For some reason, either
because it was feared that the grave might be robbed for the
valuable manuscript or because Rossetti merely wanted his poems
back, his wife was exhumed after seven years. In the light of
a huge bonfire, the coffin was opened. One can imagine the

shock felt by those present when they saw that in death Elizabeth Siddall's beautiful hair had grown even longer, until it now covered her remains. The manuscript was found, disinfected and given back to its author.

To anyone who has visited Highgate Cemetery that story will seem appropriate to the atmosphere of the place. Thousands of its graves are almost lost to view in a tangle of bushes, grass and thorns. Some of the damage to headstones and memorials is clearly the work of vandals, but to step off the paths to examine a name on a weathered wooden cross is to risk stumbling over another that has succumbed to the ravages of the years by collapsing on its back. Something is being done to clear the rubbish and the weeds, but it would take an army of workers to have much impact – and anyway there are many people who prefer the wildness of Highgate to the efficient orderliness of the modern crematorium.

Other private cemeteries which were built about this time include two in 1840 – Nunhead, near Peckham, and Brompton – and, in 1854, Brookwood in Surrey. Brompton became the first private-enterprise cemetery to be taken over by the Government. It had been built by the West of London and Westminster Cemetery Company, but was not a success. Strenuous efforts were made to economize, but the debts continued to rise while the dividends continued to fall, and the attempts to cut financial corners resulted only in a lowering of standards.

Then a significant Parliamentary Report criticized those who were using the burial of the dead as a means of commercial speculation – an interesting comment in the light of recent developments. In 1850 this led to an Act of Parliament which provided for burial grounds to be established by the General Board of Health, which could also buy those already built. This Act was repealed two years later, in favour of another allowing the establishment of more local Burial Boards, but not before the Board of Health had bought Brompton Cemetery for £74,921.

Brookwood Cemetery, near Woking, opened in 1854, produced an innovation. The owners, the London Necropolis and National Mausoleum, arranged with the London and South Western Railway that funerals would go by train, from a special siding near Waterloo Station, to Woking. There, in those unecumenical days, were developed three stations. One, for ordinary passengers, still exists. The other two do not : one was reserved for Anglican funerals; the other for 'Dissenters, Roman Catholics, Parsees, and others'.

It is now generally accepted that cemeteries may be built both by private speculation as profit-making companies and by public local authorities. One of the best-known public cemeteries is owned and run by the City of London Corporation at Manor Park. It covers 200 acres and is the largest municipal cemetery in Europe, providing a public service for north-east London and part of south-east Essex. It contains about ten miles of roads, with gardens, shrubberies and avenues of trees. The many gardeners produce nearly 120,000 plants a year, and plant 50,000 bulbs every spring. It also has a crematorium, built in 1973, which cost over £250,000. Foreign delegations visit it as a model to be followed.

Shortage of burial space has meant that nowadays more people are buried in cemeteries than in churchyards. Charges vary widely – from £7 to £48, or even higher – and there is usually a choice of grave, ranging from simple holes dug in the earth, to graves with bricked sides and floor, or 'lawn graves'. These are cheaper because a row of grass-covered graves with nothing but headstones to mark them is far easier to maintain.

Church fees for burial services are subject to a scale of maximum charges determined by the Parochial Fees Order of 1972. Having the bell tolled costs £1, and a church service about £9. Burial in a churchyard costs up to £6 plus the cost of the grave. Burial charges in a cemetery usually include the price of the grave and the fees of minister and grave digger. Headstones, for which permission must be obtained from the cemetery, vary greatly in style and cost from about £40 to over £200.

It is possible to be buried in one's garden, but permission must be obtained from the local authority and the Department of the Environment.

Cremation and Crematoria

The history of cremation goes back at least to the Bible, where there are references to the practice in both the Old and New Testaments. The ancient Romans made cremation the fashionable method of disposal, but with the appearance of the Christian doctrine attaching importance to the resurrection of the human body cremation fell into disfavour in Europe. It remained common, however, among the Indians, Japanese and Burmese.

By the fifth century cremation had become almost completely obsolete in Europe, although burning (alive) was used as a method of execution for witches, heretics and other unfortunates. But in 1960 we find that 204,019 cremations took place in Great Britain, and in 1972 375,773 were carried out in 211 crematoria. This was 57.3 per cent of 655,511 deaths in Britain that year. How this change in public acceptance came about is a fascinating story of struggle against conservatism, custom and prejudice.

Interest in cremation had begun to emerge again in 1658 with the publication of an essay by a physician, Sir Thomas Browne, called *Hydriotaphia, Urn Burial*. Six years later another book suggested cremation as an alternative to burial, but as in the campaign for the introduction of cemeteries the idea foundered on the rocks of religious narrow-mindedness.

A more romantic element was introduced in 1822, when the bodies of the drowned poet, Shelley, and of his friend, Williams, were cremated on a beach in Italy. The story seems to be shot through with a mixture of legend and reality. The bodies lay on an iron grid under which logs were piled. Frankincense, salt, wine and oil were thrown upon the burning pyre, and Shelley's heart was plucked from the flames. His skeleton was then buried in a Protestant cemetery in Rome.

Alas, the reasons for disposing of the corpses in this way were prosaic : under Italian law anything that had been washed up from the sea had to be burnt on the shore as a precaution against disease, and the iron grid had been supplied by the local authorities.

In 1869 two Italian professors, Coletti and Castiglioni, proposed cremation, 'in the name of public health and civilization', to the Medical International Congress in Florence. More papers advocating it appeared in Italy, many discussions were held, and there were several reports of practical work.

But it was not until 1873 that international interest was aroused. The impetus was provided by Professor Brunetti of Padua, who exhibited at that year's Vienna Exposition a model of a cremating apparatus he had designed and used. He was a showman as well as a physician and, as part of his exhibit, he did not forget to include the ashes that had resulted. Among the visitors to Vienna was Sir Henry Thompson, Queen Victoria's surgeon. He became the chief promoter of cremation in England. The following year *The Contemporary Review* published his paper 'Cremation : The Treatment of the Body After Death'.

Among his reasons for advocating cremation were the need for a sanitary precaution against the propagation of disease where the population was growing too rapidly for the land available, preventing premature burial(!), reducing the cost of burials, and foiling vandals by keeping the ashes in columbaria (vaults with recesses in the walls for the ashes). He also pointed out that mourners at a cremation would not have to stand exposed to rain, snow or wind. He was even daring enough to suggest that the ashes could be used as fertilizer.

The paper aroused immediate controversy, and much public and personal correspondence. Sir Henry called a meeting of his supporters at his house on 13 January, 1874. The assembled publishers, writers, artists and scientists signed a declaration that

founded the Cremation Society of England. It read: 'We, the
undersigned, disapprove the present system of burying the dead,
and we desire to substitute some mode which shall rapidly
resolve the body into its component elements by a process which
cannot offend the living, and shall render the remains perfectly
innocuous. Until some better method is devised we desire to
adopt that usually known as cremation.'

The Society was offered a piece of land in the Great Northern
Cemetery of London, but the Bishop of Rochester forbade the
building of a crematorium on consecrated ground. An acre of
land was then bought by the Society near the cemetery at Woking. In a demonstration in 1879, the body of a horse was successfully cremated. This helped Sir Henry to claim later that a
human body could be completely disposed of within one or two
hours without any smoke or smell escaping from the chimney.

But the inhabitants of Woking were unimpressed. A delega-
tion, led by a vicar, appealed forcefully to the Home Secretary.
He, fearing that cremation might be used to prevent the detection of crime, banned the practice. The Society had to abandon
its experiments.

However, in 1882 a Captain Hanham asked the Society to
cremate his wife and mother, who had both left instructions
that this should be done. Again turned down by the Home Secretary, the society had to refuse. So Captain Hanham built a crematorium on his own estate and himself carried out the wishes
of his wife and mother. When he died a year later he was also
cremated there.

All this aroused much comment in the press, but the Home
Office took no action. Then came the bizarre incident which
eventually became a turning-point for the Society. Dr William
Price, who claimed to be a Druid high priest, performing the
rites dressed in a white tunic over green trousers, tried to cremate
the body of his five-month-old son. The boy, born to the doctor
at the age of eighty-three, had been christened Jesus Christ. Dr
Price was arrested and tried. But the judge pronounced that

cremation was legal provided that the process caused no nuisance to others.

The Society could now go ahead. An application form was designed to prevent the destruction of a body which might have met death illegally.

In 1885 the first official cremation took place at Woking. Of the two others that year, one was a woman who weighed fourteen stone. Even that cremation took only one and a half hours.

Other crematoria were built: at Manchester in 1892, Liverpool in 1896, and at Darlington in 1901. But the opening of the Hull Crematorium that same year had great significance: it was the first in Britain to have been put up by a local authority. In 1902 an Act of Parliament officially recognizing cremation as a legal method of disposal was passed.

But the proponents of cremation still had to overcome the public's prejudice against the very idea. The cremation of the famous helped the Cremation Society's cause. Sir Henry Irving, the actor, was the first celebrity to be cremated before being placed in Westminster Abbey; since 1910 the practice has become the rule there. Others whose cremations were of influence have included the Duchess of Connaught in 1917, two Anglican bishops (Mitchison and Hicks) in 1923, a Roman Catholic archbishop (Dr Kurialachery) in India in 1935 (especially significant because the Vatican was banning cremation for Catholics at the time), Neville Chamberlain, two Archbishops of Canterbury (Temple and Lang), H. G. Wells, and G. B. Shaw.

The Society also published a survey in 1951 showing that more than 25,000 acres in England and Wales were then covered by municipal burial places, and a further 50,000 acres were in use as churchyards and private cemeteries. Furthermore, at the then-current rate of burial, there would be another 400 acres of land-surface covered each year. The message was obvious.

Gradually, religious prejudice was worn down and public acceptance followed. In 1961 the first crematorium was opened in Northern Ireland; two years later the Pope proclaimed that cremation was no longer prohibited for Roman Catholics, although Catholic priests were forbidden to conduct services in crematoria, until 1966. Even today, the number of Catholics cremated is not large.

Those who permit cremation include Baptists, Buddhists, Christian Scientists, followers of Krishna, Hindus, Jehovah's Witnesses, 'Liberal' Jews, Methodists, Moravians, Mormons, the Salvation Army, Seventh Day Adventists, and Sikhs. But cremation is still forbidden for Orthodox Jews, Orthodox Greeks and Russians, Islamis, Muslims, Parsees and Zoroastrians.

Before 1965 a dead person's next-of-kin could not by law cremate him if he had forbidden it. But now they can choose to cremate him or not – even if this means ignoring his express wishes.

The procedure for arranging a cremation may seem complicated by much form-filling, but most of this is done by the doctors who have to be involved before a body can be cremated. And anyway the forms' purpose is to ensure that the finality of cremation is not covering up some hideous homicide. After a disposal certificate has been obtained from the Registrar, the funeral director will provide: Form A, which is for a request for cremation made either by an executor of the estate of the dead person or his nearest surviving relative; Form B, which is completed by the doctor who attended the deceased during his last illness and who must see the body before completing the form; and Form C, the confirmatory medical certificate. This must be completed by a doctor who is neither a relative of the dead person nor a relative or partner of the doctor who completed Form B. He, also, must see the body.

These three forms, together with the Registrar's disposal certificate, will be sent to yet another doctor. He is the medical referee of the crematorium who, on the basis of the medical evidence of Forms B and C, gives on Form F the final authority for the cremation to take place.

In 1971 the Brodrick Committee (to the delight of the Cremation Society) brought out a report giving the view that these measures (applying only to cremation), including Forms A, B, C and F and the office of medical referee, should be abolished. In 1975 the Government announced acceptance of the committee's recommendations, but it will be some time before they become law.

The Cremation Society is still active. It has 10,000 members, each paying a subscription of £7.35, and operates from a country house in Kent. The Society continues to campaign actively for cremation, producing persuasive and fascinating tables of statistics. For example, 65 per cent of ashes are scattered, 17 per cent buried, 4 per cent placed in graves or niches, and 12 per cent removed for disposal elsewhere.

THE TRAPPINGS OF DEATH

Coffins

The word 'coffin' comes from the Latin *cophinus* via the Greek *kophinos,* meaning a coffer or basket. Early Greek coffins were of several shapes; some were like large urns, some were hexagonal, some were similar to today's shapes and others were triangular so that the body was in a sitting position. They were usually made of burnt clay, which in some cases was moulded around the body and baked. In the early Christian era stone coffins began to make their appearance, and wealthy Romans used coffins made from limestone, which was believed to accelerate the decomposition of the corpse.

Among aboriginals, primitive wooden coffins were formed from hollowed-out tree trunks. And after the Egyptians had progressed from preserving the body in hot sand to embalming, wood was also used. The mummy was placed in a box or boxes that developed in number and decoration depending on the importance of the dead man. A king would be commemorated in a nest of three wooden coffins, each larger than the last and highly polished or carved with hieroglyphics. The outer one would be very heavy and thickly painted with pitch, and all three might even then be placed in a sarcophagus. In Bali bodies are burnt in highly decorated towers, of which the top is an animal carved out of a tree. Lead was used for coffins in Europe in the Middle Ages, and in Britain iron coffins were common as late as the seventeenth century. Lead has also been used as a lining, as have copper and zinc.

In the United States the coffin has become dignified with another name : 'casket'. The pretentiousness does not stop there; much use is made of quilted or glass linings and baroque, gothic or jazzy styles – usually in poor taste.

A coffin has not always been thought necessary. Ever since the earliest burials, when the body was simply laid in the ground on its back, the poorest people have dispensed with them. In Britain corpses were once only wrapped in cloth or covered with hay and flowers. Now, though, the preference is for oak or elm. The Seri tribe of the American Indians enclosed the corpse between the upper and lower shells of a turtle. At the Battle of Gettysburg during the American Civil War bodies were placed in rubber sacks. In Israel today *un*coffined burial is the rule, the body being merely placed in a shroud.

Burial Clothes

The wrappings and winding-sheets of the early days have now almost completely given way to something like normal clothing, to improve the appearance of the corpse and protect it. In England before 1666 imported linen was so often used instead of wool for wrapping corpses that the English wool trade began to suffer. So an Act of Parliament that year stipulated that the dead had to be buried in English wool. The Act was not repealed until 1815, when linen came back into favour. Kings have been buried in their coronation robes, and brides in their bridal gowns. Male bodies have been buried in their own cheerfully-patterned dressing-gowns, with bright scarves round their necks. And nowadays in England night-clothes are often used instead of shrouds. Women are sometimes buried in long-sleeved night-dresses in pastel shades of pale blue, pink, green or ivory. In 1938 a woman in Oxford had her little daughter buried in all her own clothes, including a new coat, 'to keep her warm'. This would not be found surprising in Cyprus, where it is the custom to bury the dead in full outdoor clothes, including hat, shoes and gloves.

Palls

The pall that used to be spread over a coffin originated from the *pallium,* or cloak, with which a Roman soldier would cover the dead on a battlefield. Palls have often been of velvet and in the case of royalty or the rich were of great magnificence, with embroidered heraldic escutcheons, crosses, orders or decorations. Sometimes the pall has been buried with the coffin, as in the case of Charles I's black pall at St George's Chapel, Windsor. Others were works of art in themselves, embroidered with coats of arms of the London Guilds. They lent them for some funerals as a particular mark of respect. The pall of the Worshipful Company of Saddlers, which dates from 1508, is in crimson and gold. At the other end of the social scale, it was the custom at the funerals of the poor for the local authority to lend a pall. But it seems unnecessarily pointed of the Church of St John the Evangelist, Westminster, to have had their pall embroidered with the words : 'Buried at the expense of the parish'. This custom ended in 1807.

Pall-bearers at funerals were usually chosen for their closeness to the dead man in life, either professionally or personally. In the eighteenth century a head cook's pall was supported by six cooks dressed in white caps, white stockings and gloves, and green aprons.

Monuments

Monuments were known to the early Greeks, who used them to

commemorate the heroes in the national games. It was not until the sixth century BC that they began to erect *steles* in memory of the dead. These were painted or carved slabs of stone depicting the dead person or scenes from his life – a soldier, for instance, would be portrayed killing his enemy.

By about 300 BC memorials to the dead had become increasingly pretentious. In fact the very word 'mausoleum' dates from 353 BC when the widow of King Mausolus ordered a monument to be erected to her husband's memory. Located in what is now south-west Turkey, the vast white marble edifice depicting Mausolus and his Queen in a chariot became one of the seven wonders of the world. It stood for almost 1,800 years before crumbling in an earthquake in 1375.

Medieval monuments usually portrayed the dead asleep, or in paradise, or awaiting the 'last trump'; but in the fifteenth and sixteenth centuries the emphasis reverted to the more classical idea of recalling their earthly fame. By 1700, in Westminster Abbey, the suggestion of death in the monuments had for the most part given way to figures and inscriptions relating to the dead person's achievements.

This is a far cry from the epitaphs put up by some members of the modern lunatic fringe. In the United States there is a fashion (as readers of Evelyn Waugh's *The Loved One* will be aware) for cemeteries in which one can bury one's favourite pet. Among the gems of dog-loving sentimentality on headstones, collected by Barbara Jones in her *Design for Death*, are :

> SNEEZLES, HE WAS GREATLY BELOVED
> MUMMY'S OWN TOY
> OUR BABY CZAR
> GO TO SLEEPIES, BOY
> ONE EYE, SHE LIVED TO LOVE

and an animal named Bessie Bam was described as a DEAR, GOOD LITTLE WUFFIN MUFFIN. Incidentally, there is a cemetery for pets on the edge of Hyde Park in London, where British animal-lovers (and epitaph-collectors) can find similar masterpieces.

My favourite epitaph, however, commemorates a man of mystery who perished somewhere in the Wild West, presumably in its early days. He was anonymous, for the headstone simply says, DIED OF THIRST.

The heyday of the British monument makers was in the nine-teenth century, when to the Victorians it was apparently more important for a memorial to be lavish and expensive than for it to be aesthetically pleasing. Perhaps the most notable single example is the Albert Memorial, which was erected in 1872. It cost £120,000.

Another form of monument emerged in the nineteenth century. Previously, wars had been fought by professional soldiers, and in commemoration of the dead men it was the custom to put up memorials only to their generals. The rank and file had to be content with a cairn on the battlefield. But when wars were being fought by patriotic volunteers who had flocked to the colours from their homes and farms, a new kind of memorial became necessary: that which also commemorated the junior officers, sergeants, corporals and privates. This was particularly noticeable in the United States after the Civil War.

Following the First World War a rash of memorials appeared among those nations who had participated in the blood-bath. Even the very smallest villages had their granite or marble obelisks or heroic statues, with proud and pathetic lists of names under inscriptions suggesting they would live for evermore. After the Second World War it was a very different story. Partly because people felt there were already quite enough memorials, and partly because the toll had not been so heavy, there was a noticeable lack of enthusiasm for new memorials. Often the villages compromised by simply adding the new names and dates on another part of the memorial.

An interesting new development was the type of memorial which had a practical purpose, such as a club or meeting-hall which those who survived could use. Not every organization had the opportunity of the Churchill Memorial Trust, which collected nearly £3 million all over the world to inaugurate a memorial to Winston Churchill, but it then rose to the occasion magnificently. Instead of many huge, dead blocks of stone covering the nation, men and women in all walks of life are living memorials to him. The capital sum has been kept intact, and on the interest over a hundred Britons each year are awarded Winston Churchill Travelling Fellowships to broaden their professional or personal experience for up to three months in almost any part of the world.

Another example of an imaginative memorial, which gives pleasure to the living, is one thought up by the people of de Ruine Kerk, in the Netherlands. In memory of the 250 Allied soldiers who are buried in the town's war graves plot, they have installed a *carillon* of twenty-seven bells.

War memorials, graves, inscriptions and cemeteries for dead British and Commonwealth soldiers are the responsibility of the Commonwealth War Graves Commission. This was instituted in 1917 after a suggestion made by the Prince of Wales, who died in 1972 as the Duke of Windsor, that representatives of the British Empire should make arrangements for the permanent care of the graves of men who had died in the First World War. The task is enormous. In the two World Wars alone, the number of Service men and women who died totalled 1,899,188. Many of these had known and identified burials and lie in huge cemeteries near the battle areas. But more than 200,000 unidentified casualties were buried, and over 770,000 had no known grave. Others were cremated. It has been the taxing task of the Commission to find, record and maintain all the graves, or put up inscriptions on memorials, in 140 countries and territories. These range alphabetically from the French territory of the Afars and Issas, where there is a cemetery at Jibuti, to Zambia; geographically from Norway to New Zealand and from Jamaica to Singapore; and quantitatively from the 574,832 commemorated in

France to the one grave each in the Canary Islands, Costa Rica, Guatemala, Guyana, Martinique, Nepal, Puerto Rico, Saudi Arabia, Bougainville in the Solomon Islands, Togo and Venezuela.

To cope with all the administrative and practical problems, such as gardening, finding chemicals to remove lichen from headstones or protesting to foreign governments about industrial pollution damaging the graves, there was a staff in 1972 of 1,629. Of these, 1,286 were gardeners or manual workers, mostly working on the spot. The Commission's expenditure in the year ending March 1972, including wages, maintenance, plants, buildings, and repairing damage caused by vandalism or hurricanes, was over £2,600,000. Of the income, more than £2 million was contributed by the United Kingdom Government. The other Commonwealth Governments contribute according to their proportion of the numbers of dead.

The work of the Commission, whose headquarters are in Marlow Road, Maidenhead, will never be finished, it seems. Although the First World War ended over half a century ago, remains of casualties continue to be found on old battlefields. In one recent year fifty-six were recovered and given a place in one of the Commission's cemeteries.

PRESERVING THE BODY

Mummification

The use of mummification originated in areas with a dry climate, such as Egypt, and in places where the necessary preservative materials were found, such as the salt lakes in Tibet and the saltpetre caves of New Mexico.

Mummies date back 6,000 years. Some have been found in Libya, but the best known are those that were common in Egypt about 3,000 years ago. (Tutankhamun lived in the fourteenth century BC.) Mummification then had a double purpose: pre-

serving the body to receive the soul, and the creation of a like-
ness of the god Osiris. Not only was it essential to preserve the
body as the grave was a place for rebirth, 'the mansion of
eternity', but the Egyptians also believed that through the action
of imitative magic a dead body, mummified and bandaged so
that outwardly it resembled Osiris, would be reanimated in the
same way as the body of the god had been revived after death.
It would then become ruler of the kingdom of the dead.

Earlier, to arrest decay, bodies had been buried in hot, dry
sand, wrapped only in skins or mats. In order to provide for the
physical survival of the dead, food, utensils and other objects
used in life were interred with the corpse. As the number of these
objects increased, larger graves were needed. So the corpses came
to be no longer buried in sand but in spaces filled with air –
which defeated the original purpose as this method assisted decomposition. Thus there arose the need for artificial preservation
and mummification.

The first step in the procedure was to remove the moisture
from the body by packing it in natron, a form of washing soda.
Next, the brain was removed. Then, by cutting a hole in the left
side of the body, all the viscera – except the heart – were taken
out. The body was then left for several weeks in a large jar,
covered with salt up to the neck. It was then removed, washed,
and the brain cavity and skull were packed with preservatives.
The final stage was to plaster the body with a paste of resin and
fat and wrap it in bandages. The whole process took seventy
days. In later years it became the practice to replace the organs
in the body, wrapped in linen. The mummy was then painted
with red ochre and given rouged lips and cheeks, and artificial
eyes.

Embalming

In common with all animal tissue, the human body undergoes a
natural process of decomposition after death. Bacteria and en-

zymes in the body cause a series of chemical changes in the blood, and in the fluids in what are professionally termed the 'body cavities'. If these changes are unchecked, the body will take on a greenish tinge, starting at the abdomen, and become distended through the formation of gases. Any infection will also remain active in the body.

The time for this process to develop can be from a few hours to several days after death. It can depend on the health and physique of the deceased; on the surrounding temperature, and even, it seems, on weather conditions – with thunderstorms a particular hazard. Ideally, therefore, a body should be disposed of immediately after death. But in practice this can rarely happen. The body may be required for an autopsy. An inquest may be necessary before disposal can be authorized. A proper funeral takes time to arrange. The body may have to be transported overseas. In all these cases it becomes necessary to preserve the body from deterioration – either temporarily by refrigeration, or more permanently by embalming.

One funeral director estimates that embalming is requested in some 60 per cent of cases. The ceremony of viewing the body, either at home or in the funeral director's chapel of rest, is widely practised, and embalming ensures that the body – particularly the face and hands – has a natural, peaceful appearance. In other cases relatives will request embalming simply to ensure that the body is preserved after burial – particularly if this is to be in an above-ground vault. Indeed in favourable conditions an embalmed body can be preserved almost indefinitely. Lenin in his Moscow mausoleum must be the world's best-known embalmee; and probably more of his followers have seen him since his death in 1924 than ever saw him in his lifetime. Embalmed bodies have been exhumed and found in good condition after forty years. Bodies embalmed some two hundred years ago by the anatomists William and John Hunter – using oils of lavender, camomile, turpentine and vermilion dye – have been preserved in the Royal College of Surgeons in London.

And Chinese archaeologists have recently discovered two well-preserved bodies, male and female, in tombs of the Western Han dynasty, dating back more than 2,100 years. Both were immersed in 'dark red fluid', inside the innermost of three coffins. The man, found in 1975, was in almost perfect condition, with the skin elastic and joints of the limbs still moveable.

From the funeral director's point of view, however, hygiene is the most important advantage of embalming. An embalmed body is more pleasant for his staff to handle. Cremation is a cleaner process. And if the body is embalmed soon after death, this will help to prevent the spread of any infection.

Apart from embalming, routine precautions taken against infection by those who handle bodies include the use of surgical gloves and thorough washing. When a body is known to have a dangerously infectious disease such as tuberculosis, smallpox or infective hepatitis (and also in the occasional case of infestation) the general practice is to seal the body promptly in a plastic bag and to cremate it as soon as possible afterwards.

Modern embalming is quite different from the methods of mummification used in ancient times. These were based on the desiccation, or drying-out of the body by placing it in a container which was packed with 'natron' – a powdery substance with powerful moisture-attracting properties, known scientifically as sodium sesquicarbonate. Sometimes the internal organs were removed and dried separately, then wrapped in linen and either returned to the body or stored in separate jars or boxes. Facial features would be modelled in linen which had been soaked in resin, and the shape of the body and limbs would be restored by introducing mud or sand beneath the skin.

Today, embalming is much less drastic and much more effective in retaining the body's natural appearance. Essentially it involves removal of the blood and body fluids, and then replacement with special embalming fluids which disinfect the vascular system and body cavities, and give a lifelike colour to the skin.

The embalming room at one leading London funeral firm is

a white-walled chamber about fifteen feet wide, twenty feet long, and twelve feet high. There is a long narrow window high in one end wall, and a central skylight. The floor is plain concrete. Three or four metal trolleys stand against one wall; bodies are placed on these on arrival from the mortuary or home, and covered with white plastic sheets. In the centre of the opposite wall is a large hospital-type sink with elbow-operated taps; also a draining board and flush waste. Against the back wall is a table with equipment for preparing the arterial embalming fluid: a large plastic carboy, an electric pump, and metal piping leading to two large glass containers which hang from the ceiling above the sink.

The body to be embalmed is brought on its trolley into the centre of the room. A small incision is made in the upper right arm, close to the armpit, to expose the axillary artery and associated vein. If death was recent, the blood will still be sufficiently fluid to allow direct replacement through this one point. Metal injection tubes are inserted into the artery and vein, towards the trunk. A flexible tube from one of the containers above is connected to the artery tube, and a tap is opened to allow the fluid to flow by force of gravity into the body. This flow follows the normal circulation of the blood, past the heart valves, through the main arteries and ultimately to the minute capillaries throughout the body. The other tube, in the vein, is at the same time connected to a large glass jar. To extract the blood a vacuum is created in the jar by squeezing a small rubber hand pump.

Arterial embalming fluid consists principally of formaldehyde, a preservative, and phenol, a disinfectant. Other constituents include salt solution, to remove the discolouration of the skin caused by hypostatis, or settling of the blood after death, and glycerine, to assist circulation. The fluid has a pink tint. One or two specialist makers supply proprietary fluids at about £2.50-£3.00 per gallon (plus VAT), but many embalmers prefer to prepare their own according to carefully-guarded formulas.

As the tinted arterial fluid enters, the effect can be seen almost immediately. The skin colour changes from waxy yellow to the familiar flesh tone, and veins near the surface become more prominent. The closed eyes, which tend to sink into their sockets, regain their usual position.

The other body fluids are drawn off by a similar process. An insertion is made in the chest, just below the breastbone, with a trocar – a metal tube with a pointed tip. Through this the various body cavities are first drained and then charged with 'cavity fluid' – untinted, and made to a stronger formula. As a rough rule of thumb, an embalmer will use in all about one pint of embalming fluid per stone of body weight, plus one extra pint.

If embalming takes place some time after death, the liquid constituents of the blood may have been absorbed into adjoining tissues, leaving only semi-solids in the blood vessels. This may restrict the flow of arterial fluid, which is therefore introduced at further points such as the carotid artery in the neck and the femoral artery in the upper thigh. In these circumstances blood may also be drawn off through the trocar from the right-hand (venous) side of the heart.

When the embalming itself is finished (the entire job takes about three-quarters of an hour), the incisions are neatly closed and stitched, using a surgical needle and ligature. The pharynx is packed with cotton wool. Finally, the facial features are 'set', with mouth and eyelids closed – the latter with small pads of cotton wool under the lids to hold them in place. The skin, which has lost much of its natural elasticity, can be modelled to some extent to achieve a suitably restful expression. Normally no make-up is used, except possibly a little powder on the face of a younger woman. If the skin is discoloured, e.g. from jaundice, the embalmer will not try to disguise it. Realistically, British embalming practice (as opposed to American) is to present the body as last seen in life, and not to strive for idealized artificiality.

What are the necessary qualities of an embalmer, and what

is the special attraction of the job? The aspect of hygiene seems to be a strong motivation. Embalming is referred to as a 'purifying' task, and the telegraphic code of one embalming firm is 'Sanicraft'. In some respects the work is akin to surgery, and must appeal to some who feel an affinity with the medical profession. There is obviously much satisfaction in enabling relatives to view a body which looks much as it did in life. The work of embalming is the most scientifically skilled in the entire funeral trade, and its practitioners enjoy appropriate status. And there is the satisfaction of exclusivity – membership of an established profession, fairly few in numbers, whose esoteric activities are not often open to public view.

The interests of the profession are co-ordinated by the British Institute of Embalmers, whose activities seem to follow the pattern of many corporate associations. It has a national council with representatives from regional divisions; maintains a register of students, supervises a training syllabus and holds examinations – theoretical and practical; awards the qualifications of Member and Fellow; maintains liaison with thanatologists' associations in other countries (thanatology is the scientific study of death); arranges technical seminars with slides and films; publishes a magazine *The Embalmer,* which is 'devoted to the interest, acceptance and practice of embalming throughout the world'; and holds an annual conference complete with civic reception, banquet and ladies' outing.

The training of an embalmer takes from four months to a year. Much of it is devoted to theory, including a very thorough study of human anatomy. This is especially necessary for the more complicated post-mortem and accident cases which form a sizeable proportion of embalming work. There is a school of embalming in London and another in the Midlands. Between six and twelve students a year pass through the London school, whose principal reports that the profession is always short of entrants.

Most embalmers are members of the staff of funeral firms,

practising embalming as a speciality and combining it with almost any other role from driving to senior management. There are some full-time freelance practitioners, serving a number of funeral firms as required. One, in London, reckons to deal with well over a thousand cases each year. Some others work in mortuaries. And there are even a few qualified women embalmers, some working in family funeral businesses, with at least one also qualified as a state registered nurse.

Furnishing the Funeral

In Britain, as in most other parts of the western world, the ceremonies of death are conducted by the clergy, but the practical arrangements are the responsibility of a highly specialized group of men who are part of a substantial industry. These are the 'funeral directors'.

Their premises are oddly reticent establishments with shop windows – though there is usually nothing on display except discreet curtains, flowers in vases, notices saying '24-Hour Service' and perhaps an urn or two.

A typical one in north-west London was entered through a small office. A larger room further inside was modestly furnished with several old-fashioned leather-covered chairs. They had tall backs and looked as if they had strayed in from a club in Pall Mall. Behind the desk was a door whose black window was decorated with a cross, a wreath, and the words 'Chapel of Rest'. The room gave the impression of belonging to a small family firm, and so it proved.

A balding man in a black tie, black trousers and white shirt was willing to talk about his trade. What, I asked him, was the procedure when someone walked in to arrange a funeral?

The funeral director said : 'They sit down and the first thing I do is get all the facts about the death. Where it took place, and when, and the dead person's name, and where the body now is.

Its present place isn't necessarily the same as the place where it died. Then I ask what sort of funeral service is required. If the family are Roman Catholics they usually want a mass. The other questions to be settled are whether the deceased is to be cremated or buried, what sort of grave is wanted and what price of coffin or casket. These can sometimes add a great deal to the cost. The total is usually something over £100. I'd be hard put to arrange a funeral for less than £100. But some caskets can add an extra £400. Then we talk about flowers, which they usually arrange with a florist they know, and the number of cars they need. Often they say their relatives and friends will be using their own cars, so perhaps only one car or two will be needed. The funeral starts either from here, in which case the body has been lying in its coffin in our Chapel of Rest, or from the home of the deceased or of relatives. Sometimes they ask that the body should be kept just one day at their home, but in these days of small flats it isn't often kept there any longer than a day.

'All this is noted down in our records. People stay here for anything from twenty minutes to an hour or more, but they're not usually very distressed. They've not had time to feel the death very deeply yet. They've gone straight from the hospital to the Registrar, and then to us. They haven't had time to think.

'My attitude to clients is not professionally gloomy. Obviously you can't be jokey, but to pretend to be mourning someone you've never even met is wrong. You've got to show respect, though.'

I asked if his job depressed him sometimes. He bridled at this and I got the impression that he had often been asked that before.

'No, it doesn't depress me at all. We do what we can for people, to give them what they want. We're a small family firm and we do our own embalming. One week we might have no work at all; then the next you've got to do fourteen.'

Before the funeral director has collected the body from the hospital or the house where it died, quite a lot will have happened to it. It may have been the subject of a post-mortem in the hospital. In any case, a nurse in the ward or at the death-bed will have performed the 'last offices'.

This procedure generally begins with laying the body flat and straightening the limbs. The top bedclothes are removed, except for a sheet. The eyelids are closed. If they tend to remain open it may be necessary to keep them closed by putting damp swabs on them. To keep the mouth shut, a bandage is tied round the head and under the jaw. Any apparatus, such as drainage tubes, is usually disconnected.

The nurse empties the bedside locker, making a list of the items, for which the relatives will sign when they collect them. She puts a fresh dressing on any wound that needs one, covering the dressings with waterproof strapping if necessary. She washes the body and tidies up the hair and nails. Any dentures that have been removed are replaced. A plug of cotton wool is inserted into the rectum.

The body is then dressed in a shroud – a simple garment resembling a long nightdress, now often made of disposable material – and the nurse writes out labels to identify it. One of the labels is often stitched to the front of the shroud. Another is tied to an ankle or a wrist. The labels give the deceased's name, age, religion, ward and the date and time of death. All jewellery is removed, if possible. This is more easily done soon after the death, but the wedding ring is often impossible to remove. Relatives are usually consulted about this. Then the body, wrapped in a sheet, is ready for collection.

In the case of a hospital, the body will be taken to the mortuary by a porter and eventually collected by the funeral director. Probably his first step will be to measure the body, so that a temporary coffin of the right size can be provided for removal, and the coffin proper prepared for the funeral. The two measurements taken are overall height, to which two inches are added to allow the feet to rest naturally, and the width across the shoulders.

The temporary coffin is likely to be one of several in different sizes kept by the funeral director. It is similar to a regular coffin but more sturdily built, with the wood panels either varnished or painted in a dark colour, and fitted with heavy-duty handles. The interior is painted white. Recently 'removal shells' have also been introduced. One manufacturer offers these in lightweight laminated glass fibre, with brown as the standard colour and other colours on request.

For reasons of hygiene, a funeral director will prefer not to keep a body on his premises unless the funeral is about to take place, or the body has been preserved by embalming. If death was in hospital, the body will therefore stay in the mortuary, almost certainly in a refrigerated chamber, until shortly before the funeral, or until arrangements can be made for embalming soon after removal. If death is at home, the body may be embalmed straight away; but it is more likely that it will be removed as soon as possible and taken either to a mortuary or to the funeral director's premises for embalming.

Removal from a home may involve difficult stairs or passages. In these cases a special canvas stretcher will be used to bring the body down to the temporary coffin on the ground floor. The body is first wrapped in a plastic sheet, then placed on the stretcher which is closed completely around it and secured by straps. The stretcher has two handles at each end, with another on each side. Two bearers take the stretcher at the foot, and a third man supports the head end. The entire stretcher is placed in the temporary coffin, which is taken out to the waiting vehicle – either a hearse, or a plain closed van known in the trade as a 'handy'. With a practised team, removal – even with the stretcher – will probably take only three or four minutes.

In earlier times funeral firms would make each coffin individually from their own timber stocks. Indeed businesses were sometimes known as 'Woodworker and Undertaker'; and a skilled craftsman could make and finish a coffin in the space of two hours. Today, rising costs and labour shortages have led to the almost universal adoption of mass-produced coffins supplied by specialist firms.

These come either ready-made, except for linings and fittings, or in 'sets' of sawn and planed boards, to be assembled and finished in the funeral firm's own workshop.

Oak and elm are the traditional coffin woods, and some coffins are still made from the solid timber. But these are expensive, and most coffins are now of lower-priced chipboard with a great variety of veneer finishes: oak, elm, mahogany, teak, chestnut; and even obeche, agba, utile and Japanese sen. There are also plastic veneers, with printed wood finishes; and coffins for cremation are quite often covered with coloured felt or baize, leaving no wood visible at all.

The shapes of coffins also vary to meet different preferences. The familiar body-shaped coffin may have vertical or sloping end panels. The depth, from base to lid, may be uniform, or it may decrease by an inch or so from head to foot. Other styles include the rectangular box-shaped casket; and for nuns, the rarely-seen 'St Alban's' coffin, shaped like a slice of cake, may be used to give room for the headdress.

Inside the coffin, there is even more scope for variety. Linings, too, come in 'sets', with such names as 'Kent', 'Dagenham', or 'Windsor'. The set usually consists of a base sheet, with padding beneath; two side sheets, secured to the sides of the coffin, which overlap across the body; a decorative ruffle, around the upper inside edge; a pillow; and a face-cloth to cover the head, sometimes with a tassel in the centre with which it can be lifted aside. The inside of the lid may have a matching trim. Materials used include satin, cotton, nylon and silk, in white, grey and a host of muted pastel shades; and the styling can range from the purely functional to the most daintily feminine confections of ribbons and lace.

There is no fundamental difference between a coffin for burial or for cremation, except that handles and nameplate for the latter should be combustible, i.e. either wood or plastic. Strictly speaking a cremation coffin should also be assembled without nails or screws, and its interior trim secured without staples. However crematoria are practical in these matters, and the precaution is generally taken to sift the ashes with a magnet before handing them over.

A funeral starts either from the dead person's home or from the funeral director's office. Before the lid of the coffin is closed relatives are often asked if they want to 'pay their last respects'. This means looking for the last time at the body – and is also a check on its identity.

At the cemetery the bearers lower the coffin into the grave on slings made of webbing. Sometimes mourners throw a little earth on the coffin, but they usually do not stay to watch the grave being filled in by the cemetery staff.

The procedure at a cremation is nearly the same for a burial. The coffin is placed on the catafalque in the crematorium's chapel. Whether or not there is a committal service depends upon the wishes of the next-of-kin. The coffin is then either carried on a trolley or conveyed through a wall-opening into the committal room. From here it is placed in one of several special furnaces, known as cremators. The body is not taken out of the coffin. Most furnaces operate at about 700°C to 850°C. As gold melts at 1,063°C, this leaves any gold tooth-fillings undamaged. But the latest cremators reach 1,200°C, melting the gold and dispersing it as tiny fragments.

After the cremation is complete, any remaining nails from the coffin are removed and the ashes are reduced further in a pulverizer to a fine grey-white powder. Eventually about five to seven pounds of ash is left. In the majority of cases, the ashes are scattered by the crematorium in its 'Garden of Remembrance'. The dead person's family can ask to witness the scattering – for a fee, in some crematoria. If the relatives want the ashes, they can either be handed over about two hours after the cremation or posted. In both cases there is a fee for the container and the polythene bag in which the ashes are placed for safety.

Various forms of memorial are available, including plaques, garden seats, illuminated entries in Books of Remembrance, and the planting of a tree or rosebush at the place where the ashes were scattered. The charge for cremating an adult varies widely, from about £6 to £20, depending on the crematorium. Children cost less. Generally, cremation is now less expensive than burial.

Why the term 'funeral director' instead of the more familiar 'undertaker'? Although one may seem to be simply a euphemism for the other, there is a clear difference in their meaning – certainly as used in the funeral trade. Today, 'undertaking' refers to the basic role of disposal of bodies by funeral firms on behalf of public authorities. To them falls the responsibility for dealing with the unmourned, intestate dead within their area : the derelicts, the lone ones in bed-sitters, hospitals and institutions, the people who die without relatives or friends to arrange a funeral, without a home, money or possessions, sometimes without even a traceable name.

In the London Borough of Camden, for example, some 120 deaths each year are 'on the parish'. The body is given a 'common burial' (not cremated) in a section of a municipal cemetery. If the deceased's religion is known, a clergyman will officiate. The cost, of about £50 per burial, is borne at public expense. Much of this, however, is recovered through government death grants, and the Borough also has the first charge on the estate (such as it may be) to defray funeral costs. Altogether the annual net cost to Camden ratepayers amounts to about £1,600.

Funeral directing, on the other hand, embraces the entire process of staging the funeral ceremony – something which few people would have the knowledge, or be in the frame of mind to do for themselves. A capable funeral director will look after every detail ('conducting' a funeral is the term used), and the great majority of clients are glad that he does so. The only formality which he may not carry out is registration of death.

After that, the funeral director, if required, will place obituary announcements in the papers; receive flowers for the funeral; order funeral stationery (rare nowadays); remove and in most cases embalm the body; supply the coffin; provide funeral transport; notify time and place of the funeral to enquirers; arrange the service or committal ceremony, with any printing of hymn sheets; negotiate purchase of a burial plot; provide the urn for cremated ashes; arrange for a gravestone or memorial; despatch a body, in a special sealed metal-lined coffin, to any destination in the world; counsel and comfort the bereaved; and not only supervise his own staff but act as head usher to mourners at the funeral itself.

The main working premises of a funeral firm in north London are in a mews, some distance from the head office with its interview rooms and chapel of rest. One first enters the garage, where several splendid pre-war Rolls-Royce hearses and limousines (known as 'following cars') share their stabling with a few less aristocratic vehicles. Motor transport is an important concern for the funeral director; the trade magazines are full of advertisements by specialist coachbuilders, with detailed illustrations of converted Daimlers, Fords, Austins and even Volvos. Funeral vehicles seem to enjoy a high life expectancy, and the small classified advertisements regularly offer Humbers, Sheerlines and Princesses of the 'sixties and even 'fifties.

The classic style of hearse is still widely popular, the most impressive being based on the Daimler DS420 limousine chassis. A new trend, for smaller firms, are multi-purpose adaptations of standard estate cars such as the Ford Consul or Granada. To quote an advertisement: 'With the floor-deck conversion fitted, it's an elegant modern hearse. With the deck removed and the separate interior fitments installed it's a dignified following car. Or the conversion can be removed entirely to give you a roomy, powerful estate car suitable for other specialist duties or for general business use.'

The almost total disappearance of suitable moderately priced limousines from the market has led to special conversions of larger saloon cars. The rear half of a standard vehicle is cut away, and a new centre section welded in to 'stretch' it sufficiently to allow for a division and two extra folding seats in the rear.

Hearses are of two types, according to the arrangement of the fittings. In a bearer hearse, the bier carrying the coffin is mounted centrally behind the front seat, with a single seat for a bearer on either side. In a deck hearse there are no rear seats and the bier surface extends over the whole of the rear compartment, so that the coffin can be surrounded almost entirely by flowers.

Beneath the bier or deck are usually kept a light ladder, for access to flowers on the roof rack; a folding 'church trolley'; a tackle box with hand tools (including a screwdriver for securing the coffin lid, in cases where viewing takes place at home just before the funeral itself); possibly one or two large umbrellas for rainy days; and sometimes the removal stretcher. On removal work, the temporary coffin may go in the space below the bier, or on the bier with a special cloth cover.

The bier itself is fitted with a system of adjustable stops and/ or clamps to secure the coffin during transit, and rollers are set in the surface to aid loading and unloading. The coffin is usually borne on the shoulders of three or four bearers (three are quite adequate); if well practised they will move naturally in unison, supporting the coffin simply by side pressure, and using their hands only on slopes and for raising and lowering. The sight of six or eight men 'under a coffin', each with one arm stretched across to the opposite man's shoulder, may look impressive at VIP funerals, but to the expert eye is very much a case of over-manning. The inevitable variations in bearers' height means that the coffin rests unevenly, and if one man stumbles or moves out of step against another there is a very real risk of total collapse. When conducting a funeral where colleagues of the deceased wish to pay last respects by acting as bearers, the wise funeral director will either persuade them to simply accompany the coffin, or insist on thorough rehearsal beforehand.

Beyond the garage the first impression is of coffins, coffins, and more coffins. A large funeral firm must keep a wide range to meet equally wide-ranging tastes and budgets. Ready-made coffins come in lengths varying in three-inch steps, and mostly in eighteen-inch and twenty-inch widths. They are stacked horizontally, three and four high, with temporary spacers in the screw holes of the lids to prevent scratching.

Further on, in the workshop, are stacked the 'sets' of partly-prepared timber, ready to be made up to measure. After smoothing the boards of the set, a template is used to mark out the shape of the lid and the base. The sides are curved, not by steaming as one might suppose, but by 'kerfing', a process that involves making several deep sawcuts across the inner surface at the point of curving, thus enabling the board to be bent without effort.

Next to the workshop is the fitting section. Apart from the coffin on its trestles, the impression is of an old-fashioned ironmonger's, with shelves carrying countless cardboard boxes for different linings, paddings, handles and fastenings. In the corner is a pantograph engraving machine for the coffin plates; these come in coloured plastic and in bronzed, silvered or brassed metal. When I visited, at the turn of the year, there was a handwritten warning above the machine: 'Remember New Year'.

The fitting section leads to the staff locker room, and here one is reminded that employees in funeral firms are quite ordinary people doing an everyday job. Men are changing from formal suits into overalls; there is backchat, joking, whistling. On one wall is a well-worn dartboard, on another a notice-board with routine orders and a large-scale map of London. The routes to Putney Vale and Golders Green, to local mortuaries, churches and cemeteries are all well travelled. But quite often there is a 'country job', for which everyone looks forward to his turn: it means a change of scene, time to relax, and a good lunch with the lads, on the firm.

The Funeral Industry

Many people find it hard to understand why anyone should choose to work in funeral firms; for years men in the profession were the butt of comedians' jokes and the target of much criticism imputing high prices and hard-selling insensitivity towards the recently bereaved. Understandably, they became highly sensitive of their cartoon image as lugubrious men wearing black crape round tall dark hats, often with noses shaded to represent a vinous red. This image was used to great comic effect by Charles Dickens in the 1850s. In *Household Words* he gave this supposed example of an undertaker's technique :

' "Hearse and four, Sir;" says he. "No, a pair will be sufficient." "I beg your pardon, Sir, but when we buried Mr Grundy at number twenty, there were four on 'em, Sir; I think it right to mention it." "Well, perhaps there had better be four." "Thank you, Sir. Two coaches and four, Sir, shall we say?" "No, coaches and pair." "You'll excuse my mentioning it, Sir, but pairs to the coaches and fours to the hearse would have a singular appearance to the neighbours. . . ." "Well, say four!" "Thank you, Sir. Feathers, of course?" "No, no feathers. They're absurd." "Very good, Sir. *No* feathers?" "No." *"Very* good, Sir. We *can* do four without feathers, Sir, but it's what we never do. When we buried Mr Grundy, there was feathers, and – I only throw it out, Sir – Mrs Grundy might think it strange." "Very well! Feathers!" "Thank you, Sir." '

At that time all in this profession were known as 'undertakers'; in 1935, however, the name was dropped in favour of 'funeral directors'. As we have seen, 'undertaking' and 'funeral directing' now have two distinct meanings, within the trade at least. Other, more absurd, euphemisms have also crept in, particularly on the other side of the Atlantic. In America you don't say morgue but 'preparation room'; a laying-out room is a 'reposing room'; and a death certificate is a 'vital statistics form'. Dead is now 'withdrawn'. Corpse is 'remains' (or even 'Mr X'). Laying-out is 'helping repose' (while it is interesting that what a nurse refers to as the 'last offices', some funeral directors call the 'first offices'). Ashes are 'cremated remains' or even 'cremains'. Shroud is 'robe' or 'clothing'. Post-mortem in America is 'necropsy'. Money is 'cost' or 'investment'. Mourning is 'sorrow' or 'grief therapy'. And a patient who is looking like death is said to be 'going' or 'looking to God'.

Sadly for the funeral directors, the changes of title and these anodyne phrases have not helped much. Funeral directors are certainly no longer a joke, and there are some members of the public who can point to incidents suggesting that to a man they are rapacious vultures battening profitably on other people's misfortune. Clearly, they cannot all be like that. In fact at the height of a public controversy a few years ago a woman wrote of what happened after her husband died : 'For a while I could not think of what we could do. Then the wife of an undertaker called on us.' (Note that the abandonment of the title all those years ago has been a failure as far as at least one mature lady is concerned.) 'Everything was arranged for us in a decent way. Not one penny was paid as deposit, and when the bill came it was very modest. Their kindness will live with me for ever.'

A welcome letter indeed to the sorely-pressed members of the National Association of Funeral Directors. This association was founded in 1905 and most of the 4,500 funeral directors in Britain are members. The Association's office in Doughty Street, Bloomsbury, has a modest sign on the outside wall which seems designed not to frighten intending visitors away : it gives just the initials, NAFD. The Association fixes the maximum permissible cost of a simple funeral, using only one car and a cheap coffin. In 1973 this figure was £75, now it is £97.50. But this does not include such obligatory extras as cremation and burial fees, opening graves, doctors' fees before cremation, and charges for removing the body from hospital. With other charges for items that most people demand, such as flowers, tombstones, obituary notices, memorial plaques – plus VAT on wreaths, shrouds, coffins and services – the total basic cost of a funeral in Britain can be anything from £100 to £180.

An independent monthly publication, the *Funeral Service Journal* (incorporating the *Undertakers' and Funeral Directors' Journal*) gave an example of how the charges for a funeral might be made up. The case is fictitious but authentic, as it is included in the report of a speech on 'Costing, Budgeting and Financial Control' made at a NAFD conference by Robert Glendinning, 'an eminent cost and management accountant'. The phraseology is interesting.

Arranging (inc. availability cost, attendance at house & transport as required)	£7.50
Admin. & Additional Services (inc. office work (Funl. & Acs. Depts.), additional calls or interviews, messengers & transport as required, reception & listing of flowers, distribution of flowers after, advance of outpayments, credit, other services as required)	£17.50
Removal (Handy, driver, Funeral Director plus two men if required – ten miles from office)	£8.00
Preservative Treatment (inc. embalming & use of premises)	£9.50
Use of Chapel of Rest (seven nights) inc. coffining & posing flowers, & chapel reception	£7.50
Coffin as selected	£29.20
Hearse (inc. driver/bearer) twenty miles, two hrs. from office	£10.00
Car (inc. driver/bearer) twenty miles, two-and-a-half hrs. from office	£7.50
Superintendent (inc. preparation & checking in after three hrs.)	£5.25
Extra Bearers (at £2.50 & conveyance at £1)	£6.00
Total Charge	£107.95

The *Funeral Service Journal* also includes a few items to show that funeral directors have a sense of humour – which presumably they badly need. One is a report on an offer by a religious mail-order house to send plans for the Do-It-Yourself addict to make his own coffin – or, ominously, his wife's. Of simple design, the plans suggest using pine wood, unless the coffin is first to be used as a piece of furniture such as a chest, in which case it should be of cedar, oak, maple, birch or mahogany.

Other items include a list from St Paul's, the London boys' public school, of suggestions for holiday jobs for the pupils. Among the recommendations was grave-digging, because it was 'a chance to meet new people'. And a story from New Zealand: a bereaved relative telephoned a florist and said, 'The ribbon must be extra wide with "Rest in Peace" on both sides and, if there is room, "We Shall Meet in Heaven".' The florist was away and his assistant handled the order. There was consternation when the flowers were delivered. The ribbon was extra wide and on it was the inscription: 'Rest in peace on both sides, and, if there is room, we shall meet in Heaven.'

The accusations against some funeral directors of unethical practices have included 'backhanders' for people who put business in their way, the employment of casual labour such as ambulance men and hospital workers for the same purpose, charging for four coffin-bearers but providing only three and tipping a cemetery worker a small fee to be the fourth, demanding a deposit before starting to dig the grave, excessive charges such as £68 for a headstone when an identical stone in another mason's shop cost £28, and getting a 'cut' from orders for flowers or newspaper insertions. These accusations have been deplored by the NAFD, who say that since 1965 no new member had been admitted to the NAFD unless he had passed a test of ability and had his premises inspected. The NAFD also deplored the accusations of 'tip-off' practices, and was sure that all its members would too.

An NAFD report has shown that the typical funeral director

was a one-man business – often assisted by his wife – conducting about 250 funerals a year. It was often a family tradition in which a young man could be proud that he was doing 'important work for society'. A member of the NAFD remarked that a funeral director should be a combination of family solicitor, minister of religion, and doctor. More often, however, and more prosaically, funeral directors combine the business with that of builder, furnisher, estate agent or car hirer.

However, there are signs that the funeral business is moving away from the family firm (sons are increasingly failing to follow their fathers) towards the large corporation which can afford to make big savings by, for instance, using a central fleet of cars instead of a couple at each funeral director's office. For some years the financial pages of newspapers have been pointing to the advantages of investing in such a steady industry (if the investor can be sure of anything these days, it is that people will continue to die).

The largest group is the Co-operative Society. It handles nearly a third of all the funerals in Britain. In 1972, Francis Chappell and Sons, probably the largest private operators, were taken over by Musical and Plastic Industries for £400,000.

Mr G. J. Stocker, a joint managing director of Francis Chappell, told me that the firm had begun with one branch in Deptford in 1840. 'Then it grew through the generations of the Chappell family. As south-east London developed and the population passed out of the inner suburbs, Chappell's went with it. Any funeral director's work is dependent upon population, and if you see new towns developing you must be represented there. We spread to places like Bromley and Orpington, and by the mid 1930s we were doing about 3,000 funerals a year.

'In 1950 a local mason gave up the trade, and then in Woolwich a funeral director retired, and we succeeded to their businesses. So it went on, and we set up branches in Tonbridge and Crawley New Town, among other places. But in going to a new town you have to wait and be patient. The population there is essentially young and the death-rate is very low. When we started at Crawley we were doing only about forty funerals a year. Now it's up to 300. You lose to begin with, but we're there to serve the people and provide a reasonable service at a reasonable cost. These aims can best be served by a merging of interests.

'So in 1972 the firm became a member of a public group, MPI. The industry is becoming fragmented and we are caught up in economics. It is becoming increasingly difficult for small firms to fulfil a useful function.

'I expect Chappell's will do about 6,700 funerals in 1974. We now have twenty-three branches and employ 123 men on the funeral side, with twelve on the monumental side. People who started as chauffeurs or office boys can sometimes be promoted to top managerial jobs. But anyone in this trade *must* have a sense of vocation. He's got to accept he may be called out at the middle of the night or at holiday times like Christmas, and he must know he's not going to make a fortune.'

Further takeovers by MPI include three funeral directors' businesses in London, Surrey and Kent, and the publicly quoted Ingall Industries, which it bought for £1.34 million. A director of MPI, Mr Christopher Coleman, said with frankness: 'We are in the business to make money. It is our aim to get 10 per cent of the funeral trade'. His chairman, Mr Ronald Shuck, promises more acquisitions and is proud of MPI's 'horizontal' development. In February 1974 he said: 'We bury people, we make coffins and we even manufacture gravestones'.

Other recent deals by financiers have included the purchase for about £1 million of Kenyons, a well-known name in London undertaking circles, by Garrard and National Discount and Temple Securities, and the acquisition in 1972 of the London Necropolis Group by the Great Southern Group. This transaction made the Great Southern one of the biggest funeral directors in Britain, operating about twenty branches in London, Surrey and Berkshire. At the same time Brookwood Cemetery, the largest in Britain, came into the group's ownership. The net cost was about £620,542. By May 1973, the Great Southern Group's turnover had more than trebled, at £700,000, and was confidently expected to reach the £1 million mark before long.

Many people have been shocked by all this irreverent talk of takeovers, big deals and rationalizations to make fatter profits, so that death is seen merely as a business with a healthy 'cash flow' – particularly in icy or damp weather. There are still too many people for whom it is a bitter joke that with a death grant of only £30 provided by Social Security, they cannot afford to die. No wonder they tend to accuse monumental masons of callousness when they deluge the bereaved with advertising material for headstones as soon as a death notice is published; or funeral directors of exploiting personal grief to make excessive profits.

But the masons and the funeral directors also have problems; such as accounts which remain unpaid pending probate, the declining demand for headstones in an age of increasing popularity for cremation, the cost of maintaining a fleet of hearses and limousines in spotless condition and ready at a moment's notice, the wages of staff on 24-hour duty – and the shortage of men with the necessary tact, sympathy, patience and honesty.

It seems clear that we should stop regarding funeral directors as another branch of the family, weeping with us over our loss and carrying out their work as a favour. They are doing a job like anybody else, and that means that we are all perfectly within our rights to steel ourselves to 'shop around', choosing the services of this one rather than that one; this headstone rather than another that is more expensive; and firmly insisting on the cheapest coffin if that is what we really want. The problem is, of course, that all this has to be done at a time when we are feeling dazed with grief or shock, or are faced with the overwhelming practical problems of keeping a home going. The old and the lonely are the more vulnerable here, and desperately need a competent family friend to look after the details. It may be, too, that much of the vituperation directed at the heads of funeral directors has its origins deep in a natural distaste for their job. It would be easy to see their close association with the death as something very near to having caused it. But someone has to handle bodies and bury them or incinerate them, and I – for one – am only too glad to let them get on with it, as long as they don't try to take advantage of my sorrow.

It seems unlikely that the economies brought about by the business regroupings will be passed on the bereaved. The best solutions which have been suggested would appear to be the raising of the death grant or inducing local authorities to provide a simple funeral for nothing – or both.

It is little consolation for the British to know that the cost of their funerals is considerably less than those in the United States. In 1961 the average cost of an American adult's funeral was $1,450. This was the figure given by Jessica Mitford in *The American Way of Death*. It has been estimated that of the American flower industry's revenue of $414 million a year, nearly 70 per cent is derived from the sale of funeral flowers. The designs for the floral arrangements are either merely opulent, such as the blankets of orchids for funerals of famous film actors or gangsters – or 'appropriate' – as when a film director is mourned with flowers in the shape of a movie-camera, or a pianist with a floral piano. Other floral favourites are a fish from an angling club, an empty chair, or a representation of the Pearly Gates – with the gate ajar. Nowadays, however, plastic flowers are increasingly making their appearance. Many schemes exist to lighten the financial burden; for example, the prepayment of a lump sum whose accrued interest is enough to deal with any increases in costs, or insurance arrangements in which deposits paid before the age of fifty-five are doubled at the time of death. Miss Mitford also retails a story that seems almost incredible. It concerns a woman who was trying to arrange the funeral of her late brother-in-law. She chose the cheapest redwood casket. Later, the mortician telephoned her to say that her brother-in-law had been too tall to fit into the redwood casket and that she would have to take one that cost $100 more. She protested. The mortician then said: 'Oh, all right, we'll use the redwood one, but we'll have to cut off his feet'.

What is a joke in Britain is often a reality in the States.

The Rocky Mountain Casket Corporation in Montana offers to sell caskets long before they are needed. In the meantime, they can be used as wine racks, gun racks, billiard cue racks or even rustic coffee tables. The 'furniture casket' is made of knotty pine and fir with two lids and wooden nails for only £70. The 'furniture fittings', such as wine racks, are £9 extra. An American TV station came up with a hymn tune followed by jingles advertising one firm's 'caskets which are just fine, made of sandalwood and pine'. And just to show that morticians do nothing by halves, there is the service they provide which they call 'grief therapy'. This includes selling lingerie, house-coats and even corsets for the dead, and such expensive extras as Oxford shoes, which 'reflect character and station in life' and 'provide a formal reflection of successful living'. Sometimes, though, they have gone too far. Mothers whose sons had just left for service in Vietnam protested tearfully when they received in the post advertisements from morticians with the theme of 'Keep us in mind'. No wonder that a few years after Miss Mitford had addressed British funeral directors the president of the NAFD said complacently: 'Actually, she had very few criticisms of the way we do things over here'.

Military Funerals

The Armed Forces, as one might expect, have a procedure laid down for burials and funerals. The Army's regulations begin by pointing out that it is important for the troops' morale that the dead – both their own and the enemy's – should be buried with due ceremony and without delay. There are three categories of burial: emergency, temporary and permanent. The emergency type is a hasty affair, carried out by the unit on the battlefield when circumstances do not allow evacuation of the body to the rear area. It has to give the body the maximum protection from marauding animals and looting. The grave's depth should be about three feet, and whenever possible the body should be wrapped in a blanket or a poncho.

Great care is urged in marking the body and the grave, for later identification and reburial in either a temporary grave slightly away from the battlefield or a permanent grave. One of the dead man's identity discs, worn around the neck, should be buried with him. Where there is only one disc this must on no account be removed from the body. The grave should be marked by pegs and labels supplied for the purpose. If these are not available an improvised marker or cross must be erected so that it can be readily seen. At the marker's foot there should be a bottle or can, half-buried with the open end downwards, containing a piece of paper giving details of the dead man's name, rank, number, nationality, religious faith, and the dates of his death and burial. For some reason, instructions are specific that this must be written in black lead pencil, *not* in indelible pencil.

The dead man's personal effects must be listed and put into a receptacle with one of his identity discs. The list has to be checked and signed by an officer, and sent with the effects to the field records branch. In the case of an American soldier, the procedure is slightly different. All his personal effects and one identification tag are buried with the remains. The second tag is fixed to the grave marker.

After heavy casualties it may be necessary to bury several men in a common grave, usually a trench. But the Army instructs that, if possible, the bodies of different nationalities should be buried in separate trenches. The paper inside the bottle or can should indicate clearly that it is a trench grave and the distance from the marker of each corpse.

A 'group or multiple burial' is a common grave used for several unsegregated and individually unidentifiable corpses, for example 'after an air crash or nuclear fission'.

The paper used when listing any unidentified death should give as much detail as possible, such as numbers on equipment, shoulder titles, rank badges and the fullest possible physical description, particularly dental. If possible, fingerprints should be taken.

The Army recognizes that, to save labour, graves have to be placed as near as possible to the scene of the death. But they should also be chosen with a thought towards subsequent re-burial; however it advises against roadside burials because of the effect on the morale of passing troops.

The regulations about the honours to be paid at military funerals are very detailed. No officer can be buried with military honours unless he is, at the time of his death, in the exercise of some military command or office. Nor are honours to be paid officially for discharged soldiers of any rank. But they may be as a special case, if authorized by the General Officer Commanding-in-Chief, provided that the funeral is to take place within three miles of the barracks and that no public expense is incurred, other than the cost of fuel and lubricants for the vehicle towing the gun-carriage.

Military honours may be given to men of the Royal Navy or the Royal Air Force who have died while serving, so long as there is no expense other than the value of the blank ammunition fired. In London, there can be no procession unless the military service is held either at the Chapel of the Royal Hospital, Chelsea, or the Royal Military Chapel, Wellington Barracks.

The firing of field-gun salutes for military funerals is laid down so that a Field-Marshal gets a salute of nineteen guns, and lower ranks get correspondingly fewer. There are seventeen for a General, fifteen for a Lieutenant-General and thirteen for a Major-General. Brigadiers and downwards get only three rounds of blanks fired from rifles or pistols. The size of the escort at a military funeral also varies with rank. For example, a General's coffin may be escorted by up to 2,000 troops, while a Second-

Lieutenant rates only two platoons. Any soldier junior to a warrant officer has an escort not exceeding two sections (about twenty men).

Minute guns (small signal guns) are fired at the funerals of senior officers (Generals, Air Officers, Flag Officers or Commodores who died in service) while the body is being taken to the burial ground. Generally speaking, the six to eight bearers of the coffin are of the same rank as the dead man, though the coffins of senior officers are carried by warrant officers or non-commissioned officers.

Regulations about military funerals also take in such details as the proper position for the Union Jack on a coffin. It should be placed as though the 'pike' or pole from which it would normally fly were at the head of the coffin. As well as wreaths, the dead man's head-dress, belt and sword or side-arm should be securely fixed on the coffin so that they do not fall off. At the funeral of a mounted officer or soldier, a horse is led immediately behind the gun-carriage or hearse. The dead man's jackboots are placed in the stirrups, but reversed so that the left boot is in the right stirrup and the heel is to the front. At the funeral of a Field-Marshal, his baton is also placed on the coffin. (This custom of symbolically burying a dead man's accessories and emblems with him is an interesting survival from pagan times. It also occurs in civilian life. In 1896, the coffin of Lord Leighton, President of the Royal Academy, bore his palette, with paints and brushes.) While marching, arms are carried at the 'reverse'. When there is a band, the 'Dead March' will be played. All orders are given in a low voice. The coffin is carried feet-end foremost. Before it is put into the grave, the dead man's head-dress, belt, sword and side-arms, as well as the flags and wreaths, are taken off the coffin. After the service, the firing party of a Sergeant, a Corporal and twelve Privates fire three volleys of blanks. Buglers or trumpeters then sound the 'Last Post', during which officers salute, and then 'Reveille', during which they do not.

For burials at sea, Naval regulations provide a helpful diagram showing the correct positions for everyone from the officer in charge to the piping party and the bugler. If the body is being carried on board a ship from a jetty for burial at sea, it is piped on board while officers salute and the ship's company on deck obey the command 'Off Caps'. The coffin is placed on the committal platform, from which it will slide into the sea under a Union Jack (or Union Flag, as the Navy describes it), caps are replaced and four sentries stand with arms reversed at the four corners of the coffin, facing away from it. The personal mourners go below.

When the ship is clear of the harbour the sentries are brought to the 'Stand at ease', and when it reaches the burial position the mourners are brought on deck and the officer in charge orders 'Off Caps'. The service then continues as it would ashore, except that the bearers commit the coffin to the sea.

After the volleys by the firing party, and the sounding of 'Last Post' and 'Reveille', the wreaths are dropped overboard. If the body has been cremated, the ashes are not scattered but the urn containing them is committed to the deep.

Great emphasis is placed upon the need for the urn or coffin to be so treated that it sinks quickly. If the man has died at sea the body is heavily shrouded and then sewn up in strong canvas with heavy weights. This is traditionally done by the Boatswain and the Sailmaker. The regulations point out that when a man has died ashore he is encoffined by 'an undertaker', who will need considerable advice because he is unlikely to know the problems of burial at sea. To withstand the impact of hitting the sea from the deck without disintegrating, the coffin must be more stoutly constructed than usual. This will in itself give it more buoyancy than a canvas-shrouded corpse. So it needs much more weighting. But this must be only slightly biased towards the feet or the bearers' task will be more difficult. The extra weight will also need extra bearers. It is usual to drill holes in the feet end and lid of the coffin to ensure quick flooding and sinking.

But this can only be done if the state of the corpse allows it, and its effect is often nullified by the expansion of the coffin's lining and padding into the holes as soon as any water enters.

Mourning and Grief

Handkerchiefs embroidered with black tears, mourning rings, lockets, aprons and mittens, a black satin wedding dress made for a bride whose father had died a month before : these things now provoke an awkward mixture of laughter and horror. This suggests just how far modern thinking has moved away from the Victorian fascination with, and respect for, death and mourning.

Such was the Victorians' obsession with death – and in particular youthful death, which was common because of bad sanitation and was made an object of reverence by romantic novelists – that it was estimated in 1843 that between £4 million and £5 million was being spent each year on funerals in England and Wales. Even the poor spent much more than they could afford, in order to be 'respectable' and have a 'good' funeral. The cost was an important factor; Victorian advertisements show that a gentleman could have a funeral for about £100, while a first-class tradesman's would cost £50 and an artisan's £5. Paupers were buried for thirteen shillings. These were all considerable sums.

The huge demand for the correct mourning wear formed the basis of the early prosperity of two well-known firms, Jay's and Peter Robinson, and the empire that is now Courtaulds was founded upon the manufacture of crape, the thin silk fabric much used for mourning wear. In 1876 it was correct etiquette for a woman to wear full mourning, including a sable dress and mourning jewellery, for at least nine months. By 1879 the recommended period had increased to a year and nine months. Periods of 'Court mourning', 'half-mourning' and 'quarter-mourning' were strictly laid down, each with its own fashionable degree of gradually declining bleakness. The dresses were usually heavy and hard to clean, with bothersome veils. It was often two years before a widow could wear colours again, and one can imagine with what relief; many, however, grew so used to the extra attentions paid to them that they kept to sombre clothes for the rest of their lives.

The whole family, including the children and the servants, would wear black clothes produced rapidly by the recently-invented sewing machines, and some younger children were delighted to find that at last they had completely new clothes instead of a brother's or sister's cast-offs. There were black satin bonnets, black taffeta pinafores, black silk fans, black-edged memorial cards, writing paper and envelopes, watch-chains of black silk and jet, and even special black ear-trumpets. Every aspect of life was affected by death; family pets were immortalized in bronze or stuffed as an everlasting reminder of former happy days, children's books with titles like *Death and Burial of the Three Little Kittens* were recommended juvenile reading, antimacassars appeared bearing the design of a tomb, along with samplers embroidered with lines like 'My flesh shall slumber in the ground', and tea-plates painted with grave-diggers playing cards while a grave-digging machine did the work. Queen Victoria herself, 'The Widow of Windsor', inspired everyone, brooding among her mementoes of dead people and dead animals.

The cult was not embraced by every section of society, however. A Victorian clergyman noted with indignation that the poor did not treat the corpse with awe and respect, but with 'about as much reverence as a carcase in a butcher's shop'. He thought this was due to the custom of having the body on show in the house; the children played around it, things were placed on it, and sometimes it was even used to hide the gin bottle.

The many thousands of pounds spent on the business (literally) of mourning and on tasteless memorials (a partly draped lady embracing a partly draped urn was a favourite), indeed the whole cult of death, led at last to a reaction and in 1875 the National Funeral and Mourning Reform Association was founded.

It was a straw in the wind, but gradually opinions and habits began to change, until today the pendulum has swung so far that we hardly recognize a mourner when we seen one. Even the wearing of a black tie, however briefly, is often seen as slightly eccentric. Black arm-bands, or diamonds of black material on men's jackets, seem to have disappeared almost completely in recent years. This is particularly so in the South of England; in the Midlands and the North there is noticeably more fondness for the ancient customs of drawing the blinds of a house where there has been a death, sending out mourning cards, or holding a family gathering.

Studies of mourners at various stages after their bereavement suggest strongly that in many cases nowadays even well-meaning people do not know how to treat death. People have been known to cross the street in order to avoid a bereaved person, who seems to have become tainted with death. Bereavement itself has become a social stigma. Only those who have suffered a severe loss themselves know how to help others in the predicament.

The showing of grief is often an embarrassment for both griever and comforter, and friends of a bereaved man tend to want to 'take him out of himself', instructing him not to 'dwell in the past'. Many women also seem to feel this is right: they must 'keep busy' and not give way to the 'morbid weakness' of openly expressed grief. One may grieve deeply at home, but not in public. Some find it painful to stir up memories of the dead, but most bereaved people welcome a few words of condolence and would rather remember the deceased's kindnesses, jokes, talents, strengths or weaknesses, than consign him to a conversational limbo in which listeners cough embarrassedly and change the subject.

Many English parents find it difficult to show emotion in front of their children. Death is explained in terms of having 'gone to sleep' or 'gone to Heaven'. One mother said she 'tried to make it as much of a fairy tale as possible'.

What seems to be necessary, without returning to the Victorians' mawkish wallowing in death, is some form of social acceptance of the psychological need to suffer a stage of intense grief so as to adjust to normal life more quickly. Those who do not react to their loss, or do not do so until much later, find recovery much harder. As one doctor put it : 'It is better to cry through the first night than be frightened by an unaccustomed sedative'.

There are some three million widows in Britain, and more than 800,000 widowers. Many of them want practical advice on how to cope with their new situation. That there has been a real need for this help is suggested by the success of Cruse, an organization founded by Mrs Margaret Torrie in 1959, when she herself was widowed. The bereaved are given advice on problems that are domestic, social, legal and economic as well as emotional, and are helped to be positive and outward-looking, beginning their lives again. They are encouraged to 'build bridges' into the community life around them, increasing their social circle and finding happiness in becoming needed. Men are not eligible for membership of Cruse, but can also benefit from the advice given in its publications, which can be obtained from the organization's headquarters at 6 Lion Gate Gardens, Richmond, Surrey.

Also, the Department of Health and Social Security has produced a leaflet designed to help old people who do not know what to do after bereavement.

Out of the same need, but in this case created especially to help bereaved parents, grew The Society of Compassionate Friends. It was the initiative in 1969 of Father Simon Stephens, who realized the desperate loneliness of bereaved parents when he was working as a hospital chaplain in Coventry. The parents' friends avoided them, and the seat next to the father at the factory was left empty. The parents wanted to talk about their dead child but were surrounded by a conspiracy of silence. Many parents became neurotic, marriages broke up, and other children in the families suffered from the stress. The Society is a self-help group giving comfort to others who have suffered in the same way, or those whose children have a disease like leukaemia. Its headquarters are at 109 Lillington Road, Leamington Spa, Warwickshire. It has branches all over the United Kingdom and has now spread to the United States and Canada.

Grief is an illness, and it is no help to be told to keep 'a stiff upper lip'. Many bereaved people feel they are in the presence of the deceased or have hallucinations of them. In one study of 359 bereaved people in Britain, 9 per cent believed in reincarnation. This would not be remarkable in other parts of the globe – most of the world's population believes in reincarnation – but it is a higher proportion than the established churches in the West have led us to expect.

Among the physical symptoms of grief can be anxiety, headaches, asthma, ulcerative colitis, digestive upsets and rheumatism. Major losses have even been known to precipitate more serious conditions such as cancer or coronary thrombosis. The psychological manifestations of grief can include a stage of great anger against the doctor who was attending the patient, or a renunciation of religious faith. Many people suffer from serious guilt feelings, either that they might have done more to prevent the death, or for not having loved the deceased as much as they felt they should.

Studies have shown that women pay much more frequent visits to their doctors in the six months after bereavement than they did in the two years before their husbands died. The death rate among a group of 4,000 widowers went up nearly 40 per cent within six months of their wives' deaths.

Perhaps there is such a thing as a 'broken heart' after all.

> The art of living well and the art
> of dying well are one.
>
> EPICURUS

Awareness of Dying

Do terminal patients know they are dying? Should they be told? Anybody expecting simple answers to these questions will be disappointed, for they beg other questions. Which doctor can lay his hand on his heart and swear that he is always sure when a patient is about to die? Or that all patients *want* to know, anyway? Generalizations here are particularly futile. There are statistics, of course. In one recent survey, 37 per cent of the patients knew that they would probably not recover. On the other hand nearly twice as many of their relatives knew the worst.

The medical director of a terminal home said that one Sunday the families of three separate patients said, of the patient, 'We wouldn't want her to know'. But each of those three patients *did* know. One of them, an old woman, said to the doctor, 'I must pluck up courage and talk to my son'.

Dr J. Hinton, who recently interviewed sixty patients receiving care for terminal cancer, reported his findings in the *British Medical Journal* (6 July, 1974) as follows: 'Five of the sixty volunteered that they were certain they were dying, eight thought it probable and fourteen quite possible, while thirteen spoke of its possibility but with more hopes or uncertainty. Only twenty made no spontaneous direct mention of fatal illness. This accorded with my previous experience.'

Other surveys have produced a result which seems odd: that between 80 per cent and 90 per cent of doctors rarely, if ever, tell their patients that there is no hope of recovery from their illness, whereas about 80 per cent of the patients would *like* to know the bad news.

An American doctor put the argument against excessive secrecy like this : 'The patient who knows or strongly suspects he is dying is denied the chance to discuss the fact with the one person in whom he has placed his complete trust : his physician. Imagine how it feels to a patient who reaches out with all his strength for someone to share his agony and sorrow and is told, "You're looking great." The remark is such a contradiction that the patient feels deserted.'

A nurse forcefully expressed another view to me, making some revealing comments about nursing generally. 'A nurse must *never* tell a patient he is dying. For one thing, nobody really *wants* to know he is going to die if he is at all lucid, and if he is either confused or disorientated or drugged he is not in any mental state to consider the situation. A nurse's job is to promote life, relieve pain, give comfort and hope at all times, and make sure that the patient *never* dies alone.'

But whichever figures or sources you prefer, it is safe to assume that many more patients than reveal it know they are dying. There are so many signs that even the most insensitive must have at least an inkling about the seriousness of his condition. After all, he has probably already received a good deal of treatment, which might include chemotherapy, radiation, transfusions and surgery. He may also be suffering from pain, loss of weight and overwhelming tiredness. Perhaps his doctors have been suspiciously vague about his illness, or have even been careless enough to discuss his case at the foot of his bed while forgetting that he might know some of the medical terms; or he has picked up hints from words dropped thoughtlessly by other patients. (A dying patient's hearing is the very last of his senses to go, and though he may seem totally unconscious and unable to communicate he can nevertheless hear what is being said. Nurses are careful never to give any indication that death is imminent.) Perhaps a patient has managed to sneak a look at his medical chart (not all that much of a rarity); or relatives he has not seen for years appear suddenly at his bedside; or (most common, this) the emotional control of the wife or husband may be less successful than that of the medical staff.

In one terminal home they still talk of a woman who died several years ago. She had cancer, but the pain had been controlled and she was so grateful that she was able and willing to discuss her illness frankly with anyone who wished to. She never allowed her own forceful personality to droop, and the doctors were happy to allow her freedom to live out her life in her own way. Part of this was her daily ritual of making up her face carefully and extravagantly, putting on long false eyelashes. Then, on the morning of the day she died, she looked at the eyelashes and said calmly, 'I don't think I'll need those today.'

Then there was the case of the old lady of ninety with a wrinkled face covered in the brown blotches that come with age. She told me she had been in many hospitals but preferred the one she was in now because the drugs had removed her pain and she liked the food and the nurses. I asked how serious her illness was and she said, simply, that it was cancer of the rectum. She was fascinated by the treatment she was getting, and it was all I could do to stop her showing me her operation wound.

In another bed was a younger woman with the same complaint. It was her first day in the home. She, too, had been in several other hospitals. She was reading a novel, and explained with spirit that she loved reading and was going to have nothing to do with occupational therapy such as rug-making or basket-weaving if it were offered her. Her husband had died three years before and she had no other family, except for a young nephew working in a big London restaurant. She was hoping for a visit from him, but she gave the impression of being perfectly self-contained and of having accepted with quiet resignation that this was her last hospital.

This seemed to confirm the view of the senior doctor at the home, who said that the patients either didn't know they were dying or had a tacit understanding with the staff that there was no need to talk about it.

At another hospital a doctor said, 'Just as some have a right to know, there are others who have the right to be unwilling to know. Later there may be a great deal of anger at the illness, perhaps shown by blaming our treatment. Patients at this stage may turn away in isolation from everybody. Over and over again we have seen this attitude change and people reach the stage when they are ready to meet others again, and to accept what is happening.'

The word 'accept' is one that is often heard from staff at hospitals for terminal patients. They hope that, instead of fighting against the inevitable, a patient will be able to find a way of facing it – though if his character is so combative that his way of facing problems has always been to try and knock them down, the staff will also try to accept that he must deal with his situation as he prefers. However, for most patients, acceptance of the fact that they are going to die is the last of five typical stages.

The first is a horrified denial that the bad news can possibly be about himself. The doctor must be talking about someone else, and he must give hope. For days there may be a lingering dream that something will turn up – a miracle cure, perhaps, or a discovery that the doctor has made a happy error. This stage turns to anger at the doctor and his treatment, or jealousy of fitter people. Why should he be dying while other less deserving are allowed to go on living? In the third stage the patient admits the possibility that he is not going to recover, but tries to bargain with God or the doctor for just a little more time. In the stage before acceptance he will probably go through a period of intense depression and become distressed or numb. (Modern society's relegation of the subject of death as one not to be discussed is no preparation for it.) Then, particularly if he feels that his life has been 'successful', 'meaningful' or 'not in vain', he often begins to adjust, sometimes even finding relief that all the doubts are over. He can now discuss his anxieties, and in many cases it is possible for him to get a remarkable amount out of the days that are left. In his authoritative book, *Dying,* John Hinton points out that acceptance of dying comes more easily to the elderly, though over half of all dying people acknowledge that the end is near. He also says that patients in the terminal stages are often more noble than they have ever been, trying not to show their relatives that they are suffering, and kindly sparing the doctors by not asking them questions they might have to answer with lies or half-truths.

Most doctors agree that it is vital not to lie to patients, while at the same time not taking away the last grain of hope. A nursing sister said to me : 'Sometimes I suggest to Catholic patients that they take the sacrament for the sick, which used to be known as "the last rites". They say "Is it as bad as *that* then?" I tell them it might not be but anyway it would be a good idea and would make them feel better.'

The most common questions asked of staff at hospitals for the dying are : 'Shall I feel pain?', 'Will it be very long?' and 'Will it be in my sleep?' One medical director said : 'Sometimes I'm asked "How long?" and I say, "I think it would be a good idea to make the most of this spring". In other cases when the end is very near I have to be more direct. In these circumstances when I am asked, "Am I dying now?" I reply, "Yes. It is now." It's important to let the patient say goodbye. Then there seems to be for the patient a sense of enormous peace. As one said to me, "I've had it all out with my wife. Now we can relax and talk about something else." Dying is a peace and a forgetting.'

Another doctor told me that impairment of consciousness often increased as death approached. From his study of dying patients he said that 72 per cent were either comatose, stuporous or mentally confused at the time of their death. And Professor Ferguson Anderson, Professor of Geriatric Medicine at Glasgow

University, has put it like this: 'In the hands of experienced doctors, people nearing the end of their lives are kept free from distressing symptoms such as thirst, pain and discomfort. Most elderly people slip away quietly in a sound sleep, as if to a welcoming friend.'

Before a highly intelligent businessman died of cancer of the colon in a London teaching hospital at the age of thirty-eight, he agreed to record for the hospital some constructive comments about his treatment. Listening to the tape is a moving experience. In the background to this brave man's matter-of-fact words are the busy footsteps of nurses, music from a radio, a ringing telephone and the sound of other patients coughing. He described briefly the onset of his illness after having enjoyed such perfect health that he hadn't been to a doctor for twenty years.

When he had finished examining him, his doctor was very frank, for which he was grateful. The doctor said: 'It could be a tumour, malignant or benign, and I would be well disposed to take it very seriously.' The patient described his experiences at the hospital's out-patients' department and complained that when he had a barium X-ray the plates were examined in front of himself and six students, 'but I wasn't brought into it at all. It is very worrying for people to be discussed without being any the wiser afterwards.' However, in the surgical out-patients' department he was shown the X-rays and told 'In this department we give the facts – if you want them.' He said he did and learnt that the shaded portions meant a serious situation that could well be a tumour. 'They had no comfort for me or my family. They merely thought the best thing was to get on with it as fast as possible. Would I come in that week, the moment I had got my business tied up? On reflection I found this an eminently satisfactory approach. It prepared one for the worst, and when the worst didn't happen, one was relieved.' He was full of praise for the nurses. 'They were not only efficient and kind but they could also communicate. There were people who shared one's interests.' The tumour in the lower colon was malignant, 'but it was a reasonable prognosis, and my thoughts turned to getting better'. After treatment he was discharged. Three years went by, then he had to return for further checks. There were small annoyances. He was kept waiting eight days before the consultant could see him. 'This was upsetting. He kept on saying he'd come.' At this point occurred the most extraordinary part of the tape. After recalling how very frustrated he had felt by the consultant's absence, he said 'and I was feeling that Christmas was coming nearer and nearer.' And he actually laughed.

He went on to talk of his strong religious faith, though he was 'not very diligent' at practising it. However, 'This helps me enormously. I don't feel that anything that can happen to me is of any really great significance.' He ended by saying that he was grateful to the hospital for the way it had humanized its treatment. 'I'm not really at all fearful of the processes – partly because I had enormous confidence in the people who were looking after me.'

The problem of how much a doctor should tell, then, seems to vary completely from patient to patient. Each must be considered separately and a judgement has to be made on whether he is able psychologically to stand the truth. He may say he is, but the shattering news has resulted in many cases of severe depression – even suicide.

But if a man is mature and responsible, and genuinely needs to know the truth so as to make sure his will is in order; tie up those loose ends of his business; write that encouraging letter to one of his children; clear his conscience; relieve some guilt; confess a sin . . . there is a strong case that he should be told.

There is also the problem that if the doctor, out of consideration for the feelings of patients and relatives, decides to deceive patients into thinking the condition is not irreversible, he may in later months find he has created a backlash for himself. The relatives may henceforward never believe anything he tells them, or even blame him for not diagnosing the true condition.

One doctor explained to me: 'My approach to the dying is entirely empirical, based on an attempt to assess the total situation – the patient, the family and friends in their particular environment, and including such variables as the nature of the lethal illness, how long the patient has to go, the need for pain-killing and anxiety-relieving drugs, and many other factors. Then I decide what to tell and how.'

Another doctor, who spent many years as a Medical Officer in the Indian Army, spoke of the Indians' fatalism and the power of the will. 'If they feel wretchedly ill with malaria or dysentery they will often make up their minds they are going to die, and they will die, whatever you do to cheer them up and reassure them. In Britain, when the patient is still capable of making adequate provision for his dependents, he could be tactfully asked if he would like to be helped to. He might take the hint. But it must be remembered that human beings possess a great strength of will, the will to live, and it would be criminal not to encourage this where it is possible without pain. Even to hint to a patient that he is on the way out when there is a slender chance of prolonging life would be wrong.'

Easily the hardest task in writing this book – though arguably an essential one – was interviewing men and women who had terminal illnesses and who would very likely be dead within a fortnight. (That was the estimate of their doctor afterwards.) Did they know? I shall never be sure. To have asked them seemed the ultimate intrusion by a stranger, a layman, into their personal affairs.

The nearest I came to it was while in the house of a tall, gaunt Irishman in Kentish Town, London. He had been a painter and decorator before being forced to give up with cancer of the lung. I accompanied the doctor from the terminal home who was treating him as an out-patient, and the patient assumed I was another doctor. It was easy to see why he preferred being in his own home. He had a family of four cheerful, noisy sons, and a petite blue-eyed wife around whom the family revolved.

She had been told six months before that he had only months to live. She still apparently refused to believe it, and made a joke of it, teasing the doctor that he didn't know what he was talking about. She was always looking on the brighter side. 'He's looking well, isn't he, doctor?' and 'He's eating very well'. The patient just smiled indulgently but was racked every few minutes with a terrible cough. She must have known the truth, but there was always hope – and in any case there was no harm in having a laugh. It was a warm, easy relationship.

Care of the Dying

Patients with poor or distant prospects of recovery have never been popular in hospitals. The hospitals see their role as a *curing* one; they do not have the facilities, the staff or the time to give prolonged care to those who are beyond hope. This is not a satisfactory situation, but it is understandable. For such patients, then, there is the choice of living out their last days at home, cared for by their families (if this is possible), or of being admitted to one of the hospitals – there are now more than thirty in Britain – that specialize in treating and relieving symptoms rather than going all out to cure the disease causing those symptoms.

The choice is not an easy one. There are advantages and disadvantages in both options. The hospital has the skills, the drugs and the facilities to relieve pain; the problems of caring for a seriously ill patient at home are many and difficult, involving the cost and organization of extra laundry and night nurses, not to mention the emotional strains on the family itself. The home, however, has the advantages of familiarity, of loving affection, and the very fact that it is *home* and not an institution, however kind and caring that institution may be.

Perhaps the answer is to combine both options when this is possible. Various nerve-blocking procedures can be used to achieve pain relief, often enabling a patient to return home and stay there comfortably. Treatment centres have out-patient departments which send doctors and nurses to care for patients in their homes. In one case a young woman tried to commit suicide at home when she realized the seriousness of her illness. The attempt failed and she was admitted to hospital. But once her pain and vomiting were controlled she went back to her family. She was able to see her children growing up for another year, for which she and her husband were more than grateful. When she returned to her bed for the last time they both kept repeating to the doctors: 'The children are a year older'.

There are a number of organizations that can help with advice and practical aid if the patient and his family do opt to stay at home, but it is essential that they are told that this help is available and where to find it.

Sheila Hancock, the actress, had to cope at home with two personal disasters, one after the other. Only a month after her mother died from cancer, she was told that her husband also had the disease. At a symposium on the care of the dying, held at the Royal College of Physicians, she told the audience of doctors, nurses, administrators and social workers that when she first began looking after her mother she had a feeling of total bewilderment: 'Having no experience of illness I desperately wanted to learn how to take care of my mother and you do not, as an actress, know how to deal with bedsores and enemas and suppositories and things like that. But I found a strange resistance in some of the district nurses to teach me.'

Doctors were similarly unhelpful. Their training was geared to curing; dying was seen as a failure. When the time came for her mother to have pain-killing injections, it was a terrifying situation: 'I could not phone my GP at all hours of the night, there was no 24-hour service as far as I knew, and in fact I was often left in the middle of the night with my mother in absolute agony, not knowing where to turn. I know now that there were places that could have helped me, but I did not at the time.'

She found a great lack of information about the facilities available to her. 'Maybe I just slipped through lots of loopholes in some way, but I didn't know about the Red Cross and the things they could supply. I didn't know about the million and one things that are available. I didn't even know, believe it or not, about the Marie Curie Foundation until after my mother had died. It seems to me that there is some deficiency here. You should be referred to people who can give you the information that can help you, and I think it is too difficult for a busy GP to cope with all that.'

In her husband's case, things were very different. She was referred to a specialist home for cancer which believes strongly in the benefits of home care where possible. Its proportionately large staff of doctors and specialists keeps in close touch with its out-patients. And, says Miss Hancock, 'I was taught with loving care to look after my husband, and I think it was considered that the more I could do for him the happier they were.'

In her dressing-room at the Criterion Theatre, she told me that she was still working to get better facilities for the dying. 'Facilities are woefully inadequate and some GPs don't know what is available. They should have more specialized knowledge of dying and of drugs. Some have unpleasant side-effects, like constipation. For home help there's a need for a special corps of nurses or doctors on a 24-hour service. At the terminal home my husband was in, they knew all about drug control. It was more like a club than a clinic.'

The root problem seems to be one of insufficient staff. Local authorities and voluntary societies such as the Red Cross, the National Society for Cancer Relief and the Marie Curie Memorial Foundation between them provide some nursing care, health visitors, meals, domestic help, special laundry services and night nurses. But it is not easy to recruit for these tasks, and in many parts of Britain the services have to be supplied by willing but over-stretched part-time workers.

Some useful addresses for people who find themselves in the

same situation as Miss Hancock may be found at the end of this chapter.

The Marie Curie Memorial Foundation and the National Society for Cancer Relief also run centres specializing in caring for terminal patients. Others are run by religious foundations, like the Irish Sisters of Charity, or by registered charities. Perhaps the most famous of these centres is St Christopher's Hospice in Sydenham, London. St Christopher's is the model upon which many other centres in Britain and abroad have been based, and its medical director, Dr Cicely Saunders, is one of the leading world authorities on this branch of medical care.

The Hospice has fifty-four beds and most are occupied by patients with illnesses that involve chronic pain. But no one there is in pain. Dr Saunders and her staff use analgesics to *prevent* pain occurring, rather than to control it once it appears. The aim is to administer pain-killing drugs – often simple and familiar ones like aspirin, paracetamol or codeine – so that they are one step ahead of the pain, instead of one step behind. Narcotic drugs like morphine and diamorphine are also used, but they are not administered in massive doses so that the patient is in a permanent, semi-comatose state; rather they are geared to each patient's needs, with care being taken to ensure, where possible, that the drugs do not interfere with his personality or capability for physical activity.

Doctors at less advanced centres often hesitate to use morphine or related drugs, on the ground that the dose might have to become greater and that the patient could become addicted. But in terminal illness these fears are unjustified. At one centre between 90 and 95 per cent of patients needing diamorphine never have more than a 30 mg dose. As for addiction, patients do not develop a craving for the drug when they no longer have to crave relief from pain. But in less enlightened places, where the drug is given only on the basis that the patient must endure an hour or more of agonizing pain before the next, equally inadequate dose, the development of craving is understandable.

One patient complained that he had been 'in agony for three months'. Carefully examined, he was found to have intensely tender ribs. Even to breathe hurt him, and any movement produced whimpers of misery. His general practitioner had kept him on opiates for three months but had insisted on a low dose for fear of addiction. Two days later, properly treated, he was relaxed and smiling.

Diamorphine is often preferred over morphine for several reasons; it causes less nausea, often produces a return of appetite, is less constipating and improves the patient's morale and alertness. It is the standard treatment at most terminal centres, although it is currently being reassessed at one centre. It is usually given orally, as part of a mixture which also contains cocaine, syrup, chloroform water and – this may be a surprise – 95 per cent ethyl alcohol. Other versions of the same 'cocktail' contain honey, and gin. As one doctor said : 'Alcohol is one of the best sedatives that exist for terminal patients and an excellent help in the control of pain. They should be allowed all the alcohol they want.'

But the centres do not claim that morphine and diamorphine are panaceas for terminal pain. One per cent of patients get only slight relief, and a further 20 per cent fail to get complete relief. The best dose of medicine at a terminal centre is simply that which keeps the patient free of pain, given regularly every four hours – even two-hourly if necessary. As Sir Stanford Cade pointed out in his Nuffield Lecture in 1962, the fundamental question is : 'What is the relative value of the various available methods of treatment *in this particular patient* ?'

Good nursing and a pleasant, cheerful atmosphere are obviously of immense importance. In her aptly titled article on St Christopher's ('A Very Nice Place', *New Society,* 12 December, 1974), Mary-Kay Wilmers wrote : 'I myself expected to find St Christopher's extremely depressing : it wasn't at all. The building itself is not lugubriously plush like some private nursing homes, but clean, neat and bright, rather like a school. It's situated in a leafy residential street. There are flowers in the windows and open days for the local community. The wards are divided into bays of six or four beds, and some patients have single rooms. Most of those I saw were sitting up and many were out of bed. If you compare a terminal patient at St Christopher's with a terminal patient elsewhere the difference is striking. "Yours don't look as terminal as ours do", I heard a nurse from another hospital say in bewilderment.'

Patients are continually encouraged to feel that their lives are still worth living. Visiting is allowed at almost any time, children are encouraged to visit, and cats and dogs can be brought in. Young patients are given single rooms so that they can sometimes be alone with their girl friends or boy friends. Parties are held on birthdays or special occasions.

The nurse-patient ratio is exceptionally high; for every four patients there are five full-time nurses. And the solution to the perennial problem of how much a seriously ill patient should be told of his condition is typically simple and effective at St Christopher's. Among every patient's notes there is a sheet for recording his own comments on his illness, so there can be no doubt about how much he knows.

St Christopher's Hospice is a registered charity rather than a state hospital, but the NHS pays three quarters of the running costs. The remainder, approximately £80,000 a year, is raised in private donations. Patients' families contribute towards the cost of their stay, if they can, but 'no one is kept in or out on grounds of money', to quote Dr Saunders. On average the Hospice receives £5 a week from each patient.

The quality of care is maintained up to and even after the patient's death. Mary-Kay Wilmers writes: 'It's clear from listening to the doctors talk about the patients that they allow themselves to become more interested in them, and closer to them, than doctors inside or outside hospitals ordinarily do. I asked how they cope with patients who have no family. It isn't a problem: there's always someone on the staff with "a weakness for little old men who smoke in bed". When a patient who has been there a little while dies, the staff who have been looking after him usually go to his funeral, and one of the doctors explained that they are frequently able to help bereaved relatives simply by showing that they themselves are upset at a patient's death. If the doctor puts his arms around the patient's wife or has tears in his own eyes, it enables her to express her own grief.'

St Christopher's is outstanding even among the centres specializing in the care of terminal patients, and obviously one cannot hope that the standard of care found there can be matched by every terminal ward in every general hospital in Britain. However, if every hospital were to treat the dying and those in pain with even a little of the compassion, the concern and, above all, the cheerfulness one finds at St Christopher's, the 'last illness' would not be the painful, lonely and humiliating affair it too often is at present.

Some Useful Addresses

The following organizations can provide advice and help in the care of a seriously ill person at home :

The British Red Cross Society, 9 Grosvenor Crescent, London SW1.

The Marie Curie Memorial Foundation, 124 Sloane Street, London SW1. (A charitable organization which can help to provide, in conjunction with the district nursing officer, the services of a night nurse for one or two nights a week, as circumstances warrant. The Foundation also runs twelve nursing homes. Their concern is with *cancer patients only*.)

The National Society for Cancer Relief, 30 Dorset Square, London NW1.

For elderly patients in need of nursing home care the following organization can give advice and help :

The Elderly Invalids Fund, 10 Fleet Street, London EC4. (A charitable organization that can provide subsidies to enable elderly invalids to have care in private nursing homes, or relatives to take a rest from nursing a patient at home by arranging alternative cover for short periods. Their concern is with women patients over sixty and men over sixty-five years of age.)

> The world recedes; it disappears;
> Heav'n opens on my eyes; my ears
> With sounds seraphic ring;
> Lend, lend your wings! I mount! I fly!
>
> ALEXANDER POPE

'Why did you bring me back, Doc? It was so nice there.'

This aggrieved comment by an American hospital patient was made, surprisingly enough, after he had been revived from a condition very near to death. Another patient, on whom the medical staff had just wrought a near-miracle of resuscitation, was similarly ungrateful. 'I want to go back,' he said. 'Let me go back.'

Such remarks from very sick people who have 'returned from the dead', are not as rare as one might expect. They have had visions that surprised and delighted them, and it would be a pessimistic man indeed who could not find in this a crumb of comfort. Many people have 'lived to tell the tale' – lucidly.

While collecting honey from hives in Derbyshire, thirty-three-year-old Bill Askey was stung on the neck by a bee. His hands went blue and his breathing stopped. His brother, Max, felt his heart but that had stopped too. Max massaged it for three minutes before Bill began breathing again. After two days in hospital, Bill was asked what it had felt like to be 'dead'. He replied, 'It's like falling gently through space.'

Peter Sellers, the actor, has described his sensations during a heart attack in 1964. 'I felt as if I was dozing off and then waking up. But each time I had slept I had, in fact, died. My heart had stopped. I didn't feel as if I were dying. If that's what dying's like, then I shan't worry about it again.'

Lady Howard de Walden, who was allergic to ether, was given some when she was giving birth to her daughter. In her autobiography she described what happened. 'The doctors just would not listen and plumped an ether mask on my face. And so I died. They had the dickens of a job resuscitating me, and afterwards I was almost glad to hear that, while coming round, I bit the anaesthetist's finger to the bone. Whilst I was dead it seemed that I was beyond all space, which was without light. I was being gently held while deep golden voices spoke. I could not turn round, because the Lord of all Creation was (though aeons away) behind me; but right and left I could glance through coloured vastness. Violent colours, though there was no light. I was asking questions and it was explained to me that goodness and music helped towards the creation of light. Then a great ringing of soundless bells and I was told of the change of plan and I was to go back. I did not want to go, and as I sank and became diaphanous, their voices followed me, saying, "Remember . . . remember!" '

She then regained consciousness, the centre of attention for a group of conscience-stricken doctors. Her daughter had been born safely.

Weil's Disease is a rare but usually fatal malady that is caught from drinking infected water. Joe Hyams, the author, caught it in Spain. For four days he had a fever, his temperature fluctuating between 102° and 106°. Later he described his death experience as 'blissful'. He had been in agonizing pain, but it disappeared and he began to feel happy. He was in a euphoric state – smiling, humming and singing. Then he gradually became aware of his wife telling him, over and over again, not to go to sleep. He wanted to, but he realized she was asking him not to die. He knew he was dying and if he let himself drift it would be the end. He attributed his recovery to this.

The need to make this deliberate act of will to survive during a critical period is common to many of these experiences. Robert Chetwood described to me what happened when he suffered a pulmonary embolism. 'The pain was excruciating, as any doctor will tell you, but I fought hard against it though accepting it, not wanting to make a fuss. I must have been unconscious, as I heard and saw nothing in the ward.

'Gradually the pain began to disappear and I experienced a wonderful feeling of drifting as on a cloud, no pain, just drifting upwards. The speed of my ascent seemed to increase, like being caught in an upward draught. All around me was a darkness and I got very scared. Something within me urged me to open my eyes: "Fight against it. You *must* fight against it". I did this, but I don't know how.

'I heard a plate rattle in the ward somewhere, and somehow I opened one eye and saw the white ceiling. At once the excruciating pain returned, and very soon my bed was surrounded by hospital staff.

'I'm not afraid of dying now, as it is a very peaceful affair.'

A bed-ridden woman who said she had 'died three times' impressed me with her cheerful attitude to life. 'I've been pronounced "incurable" after several high blood-pressure seizures which damaged my brain, heart and kidneys. At the same time I had pleurisy and pneumonia.

'The first time I "died" was twenty years ago. I felt very ill and I remember saying, "Oh, I'm dying". But what amazed me was that I was *not* thinking of God. I'd been a practising Christian for many years, but had grown rather disillusioned.

'One of my kidneys was taken out, as well as some nerves and blood vessels. I was in hospital nearly six months, my brain wasn't functioning and I was a cabbage. But I was determined not to give up, because I had two children and I just had to look after them. I had a great fear of dying alone. In time, my brain recovered.

'The next time I collapsed was a year later. It was a marvellous feeling while I was dying, like being on a cloud. But there was a voice inside me saying: "You mustn't die".

'Again I collapsed at a bridge party, and in hospital I was

again pronounced to be dying. Now I spend nearly all my time in bed. But I'm no longer afraid of dying and I'm enjoying life. I play bridge often with friends who sit beside my bed, and I spend a lot of time trying to help other people who are afraid of dying. One old lady said she was very afraid. I talked to her for a long time. She died a few days later, and I was told that she died very contentedly.'

In a survey conducted by doctors and psychiatrists at the Central Middlesex Hospital, London, one of twenty patients who had suffered cardiac arrests said that during the period his heart had stopped he had heard angels singing. Another, who was thought to be dead at the time, definitely heard someone say, 'My God, his heart has stopped.' Twelve of the patients realized that they were momentarily dead. Two said that they were no longer frightened of death as a result of their experiences. Several remembered being aware that people were giving them cardiac massage, which surprised the doctors.

The curious sensation of floating above their own bodies, observing dispassionately what was being done to them as if they were strangers at their own bedsides, is an experience reported by several people.

Frederick Priest was taken to the intensive care unit at a hospital in Worcestershire, to have electric shock treatment for his heart, which had stopped. As if miles away, he saw the doctors and nurses rushing about his bed. Then a priest arrived to give the patient the last rites, and it was with some surprise that he realized the patient was himself. All the time he felt remote, detached from the feverish activity.

Similarly, Mrs Olga Jalink, in a Pembrokeshire hospital, felt she was looking down at herself from 'an in-between world'. Everything was silent and tranquil. Now she has no fear of dying and is quite sure that there is some form of existence after death.

A policeman was in the same situation after a car accident. He could see a girl pulling a policeman from the wreckage of a car and giving him mouth-to-mouth resuscitation. He wondered why he, a policeman, was doing nothing to help. When he saw the face of the man was his own he 'could have dropped down dead'.

During a crisis with jaundice, David Reading felt he was floating on the ceiling, looking at his body on the bed. 'There was no sound whatsoever. It was like being in a vacuum. I was told later that I was shouting at the top of my voice, "I don't want to die." And yet I heard nothing, nor anything of the people around me. It was a most strange and wonderful experience. How easy it must be to "pass over", one half of the body going and one half desperately wanting to stay. I do feel that people who have partly experienced death imagine more than they see, or are allowed to remember.'

A very matter-of-fact view was taken by Mrs Pamela Large, who nearly died from a large embolism in an artery eighteen years ago. She told me : 'It was shortly after I had given birth to my son. I suddenly felt everything recede from me. I knew I was dying. Luckily, a nurse came in with my lunch. She said afterwards that my lips had gone blue. She rushed out, and I heard her calling for the matron. My whole life was ebbing from me. It was a great sadness. I was going to leave everything I knew and loved. It was the most lonely experience anyone can have. But I knew God was there, though not in a hysterical way. I saw no God-like figure, nor hallucinations, nor magnificent apparitions. It was all extremely matter-of-fact. I was returning to somewhere, going on an enormous journey, and I knew where to. I was going back to more beauty and more pure goodness than it is ever possible to know here.

'I was above my body and I could see everyone. Matron came in and felt my pulse. I was told later that she said to the nurse, "It's no good. She's gone". But I was too far gone to hear that. I think what brought me back to life was a prayer, not for myself but for my children. I prayed, "Please, God, don't let me die, for their sakes". Soon after this I realized I was back

in bed and felt tremendous pain. I was in the nursing home for
nearly five months.

'Until that experience I had feared death and hadn't been
very religious. But since then my life has changed. I don't have
any orthodox religion, but I go to meetings of local Quakers.
And I'm not afraid of death any more. My religion is not
treacly, sickly or sentimental. I just don't bother now with
futile quarrels or worry about life's ups and downs. If I had to
die tomorrow I'd feel very much alone, but not afraid.'

J. H. Magoon attributes his return from death to a remark-
ably similar prayer. He had been involved in an accident when
a nylon moulding machine exploded and covered one side of
face with molten nylon. A few days later he suffered a heart
collapse. 'My eldest child slept at the hospital (I was a widower
at the time) and was told the worst had happened. A mortuary
attendant was at hand to remove me, I was told afterwards, and
I remember a priest reciting a hymn of rites and I went down
and down into depths with no chance of ever seeing the very
bottom. I also remember praying to God to help me return
for my children's sake, then feeling a warm hand on my shoulder
and features such as I have always imagined God to be like,
comforting me. A lady doctor stayed with me the whole of that
night, giving me injections. When I did recover, not a muscle
functioned, but I knew that now with faith I would be able to
fight to live again. It took some years to feel well again, and a
great deal of treatment. I am sixty-one now, and although I
don't go to church I believe and always say prayers hoping that
the same help will be given to all the people who need it.'

Other people have described these awesome moments as 'going
into nothingness' or 'fading out like lights'. Some felt as if their
bones were made of rubber or had the sensation of life flooding
suddenly into them. To a few being almost dead was 'just like
fainting – total blackness. A black abyss', or 'It was as I had
expected it would be – nothingness'.

A study of the visions seen by patients on their death-beds, carried out by the Parapsychology Foundation of New York, suggests that this 'nothingness' is far from typical. Several of the 35,000 patients observed told doctors or nurses that they had seen 'The Promised Land' or 'a beautiful city' or 'birds with brightly lighted eyes or tails flying in a jumbled circle'. A six-year-old boy described having seen Heaven : a beautiful land with many flowers, and birds singing. Nearly all the people who saw visions died within a day.

But hallucinations in which human beings were seen more often than landscapes were more common. It was found that the dying usually hallucinated religious figures or people who were already dead, whereas the living saw or heard the living. The most frequent hallucinations were of the patients' parents and children, followed in order of frequency by their friends, God, saints, prophets, Jesus and angels. Surprisingly together at the end of the list were 'The Virgin Mary' and 'devils'. Visions of the latter were dramatic, and one patient saw himself being attacked with red-hot pitchforks. At the other end of the heavenly scale, a patient claimed he had 'shaken hands with the Lord'.

Some hallucinations were simply the patient's relived memories. Others saw apparitions of familiar visitors to the hospital; most seem to have been friendly, sympathetic, or wanting to take the patient away to another and better existence. At other times the apparition forbade the patient from 'passing on', as in the case of the man who heard and saw his father tell him : 'No, not now, Willy, not now'. Two-thirds of those who saw hallucinations died within twenty-four hours. And several nurses and doctors reported that some patients died immediately after their hallucinations. One patient said, 'Now, Ann, I am coming' – and promptly died.

Often, patients suddenly opened their eyes wide, staring at something very surprising, almost reaching out. In another survey, a man who was delirious and in great pain suddenly became calm and his face lit up. 'Oh,' he cried joyfully, 'the Light! the Light! Oh, there's Annie – and John!'

A more curious incident, this time from England, concerned a dying woman who, to avoid distressing her, had deliberately not been told that her sister had died a fortnight before. The dying woman said: 'It is all so dark, I cannot see'. A moment later her face brightened and she exclaimed: 'Oh, it is lovely and bright. You cannot see as I can.' A little later she said: 'I can see Father. He wants me; he is so lonely.' Then, with a rather puzzled expression, she said that her sister was with him. She died a few minutes later.

The age or sex of the patient seems to have had no effect one way or the other, and patients were not heavily sedated at the time of the hallucination. Sceptics who would put all this down to the powers of sick imaginations may be impressed by the case in which the same hallucination was seen by both patient and nurse. The figure was the patient's old sister. The nurse was efficient enough to write the incident down in her notebook. In a similar case a nurse was sitting at the death-bed of her own husband when she saw 'people dressed like they were at Christ's time fade through the wall'. Later, her husband astonished her by describing what he had seen. It was the same scene.

Interesting statistics are given in the American report on the effect of the hallucinations. Most of the patients who had one were afterwards peaceful and calm; only a few had been frightened by them. About 42 per cent were indifferent to their approaching end; 18 per cent showed fear or panic, while 5.5 per cent were definitely excited, even exalted. Less than 10 per cent were conscious during the last hour. Unexpectedly, two cases of senility and schizophrenia regained their normal mentality just before death.

To conclude, I spoke to two doctors with much experience of observing dying patients. They were reassuring about the end most of us can expect. One said that even when the patient had become increasingly anxious for days, he became much calmer in the last one to three hours before death. Another put it this way: 'There is such a resigned, peaceful, almost happy expression which comes over the patient – it is hard to explain but it leaves me with the feeling that I would not be afraid to die.'

BIBLIOGRAPHY

Unless otherwise stated the place of publication was London.

Agate, J., *The Practice of Geriatrics,* Heinemann, 1963.

Ariès, P., *Western Attitudes Towards Death,* Johns Hopkins University Press, 1974.

Barker, J. C., *Scared to Death,* Frederick Muller, 1968.

Barrett, W., *Deathbed Visions,* Methuen, 1926.

Bendall, E. R. D., and Raybould, E., *Basic Nursing,* H. K. Lewis, 1970.

Brodrick Committee, *Death Certification and Coroners,* HMSO, 1971.

Brooke, B., *Understanding Cancer,* Heinemann, 1971.

Caldwell, J. R., '100 Deaths in Practice', *Journal of the Royal College of General Practitioners,* August 1971.

Care of the Dying, Proceedings of a National Symposium, HMSO, 1972.

Carruthers, M., *The Western Way of Death,* Davis-Poynter, 1974.

Cartwright, A., Hockey, L., and Anderson, J. L., *Life Before Death,* Routledge & Kegan Paul, 1973.

Commonwealth War Graves Commission, *53rd Annual Report,* HMSO, 1972.

Consumers' Association, *What To Do When Someone Dies,* rev. ed., 1973.

——, *Wills and Probate,* rev. ed., 1975.

Cremation Society, The, *Directory of Crematoria in the British Isles,* Maidstone, published annually.

Cunnington, P., and Lucas, C., *Costume for Births, Marriages and Deaths,* A. & C. Black, 1972.

Curl, J. S., *The Victorian Celebration of Death,* Newton Abbot, David & Charles, 1972.

De Walden, M. H., *Pages from My Life,* Sidgwick & Jackson, 1967.

Downie, P. A., 'Terminal Care', *Nursing Times,* February 1973.

Downing, A. B. (ed.), *Euthanasia and The Right to Death,* Peter Owen, 1969.

Emery, J. L., and Marshall, A. G., *Handbook for Mortuary Technicians*, Oxford, Blackwell, 1965.

Evans-Wentz W. Y. (ed. & trans.), *The Tibetan Book of the Dead*, Oxford University Press, 1968.

Exton-Smith, A. N., 'Terminal Illness in the Aged', *The Lancet*, 5 August, 1961.

Feldman, S., and Ellis, H., *Principles of Resuscitation*, Oxford, Blackwell, 1967.

Felstein, I., *Later Life : Geriatrics Today and Tomorrow*, Harmondsworth, Pelican, 1969.

Galpin, C., *The Search for Youth*, Corgi, 1968.

Gorer, G., *Death, Grief and Mourning in Contemporary Britain*, Cresset Press, 1965.

Halsbury, Earl, *Halsbury's Laws of England*, Butterworth, 1956.

Harrington, A., *The Immortalist*, Panther, 1973.

Hinton, J., *Dying*, Pelican, 2nd ed. 1972.

Hughes, G., *Peace at the Last*, Calouste Gulbenkian Foundation, 1960.

Jones, B., *Design for Death*, Deutsch, 1967.

Kastenbaum, R., and Aisenberg, R., *The Psychology of Death*, Duckworth, 1974.

Kluge, E.-H. W., *The Practice of Death*, New Haven, Yale University Press, 1975.

Kübler-Ross, E., *On Death and Dying*, Tavistock, 1970.

Lewis, O., *A Death in the Sanchez Family*, Penguin, 1972.

Lifton, R. J., and Olson, E., *Living and Dying*, Wildwood House, 1974.

Lockyer, H., *The Funeral Source-Book*, Pickering & Inglis, 1967.

Lynch, P. P., *No Remedy for Death*, John Long, 1970.

McLachlan, G. (ed.), *Portfolio for Health, 2*, Oxford University Press, 1973.

Mason, F., and Windrow, M., *Know Britain*, George Philip, 1972.

Medical Research Council, *Annual Reports*, HMSO.

Mitford, J., *The American Way of Death*, Hutchinson, 1963.

Morley, J., *Death, Heaven and the Victorians*, Studio Vista, 1971.

Nelson, J. E., *Spiritualism for Beginners*, Spiritualist Association of Great Britain, 1965.

Osis, K., *Deathbed Observations by Physicians and Nurses*, New York, Parapsychology Foundation.

Parkes, C. M., *Bereavement*, Tavistock, 1972.

Pirie, D., *A Heritage of Horror*, Gordon Fraser, 1973.

Prescott, F., *The Control of Pain*, English Universities Press, 1964.

Proceedings of a Conference on the Problems of Euthanasia, in *Documentation in Medical Ethics, No. 1*, London Medical Group and The Society for the Study of Medical Ethics, 1972.

Purchase, W. B., and Woolaston, H. W., *Jervis on Coroners*, Sweet & Maxwell, 1957.

Rees, W. D., 'The Distress of the Dying', *British Medical Journal*, 8 August, 1972.

Saunders, C., *Care of the Dying*, Macmillan, 1960.

St Christopher's Hospice, *Annual Report 1971-2*.

St John Stevas, N., *The Right to Life*, Hodder & Stoughton, 1963.

Shibles, W., *Death : An Interdisciplinary Analysis*, Wisconsin, Language Press.

Special Panel of the Board of Science and Education, 'The Problem of Euthanasia', *British Medical Journal*, 23 January, 1971.

Stephens, S., *Death Comes Home*, Mowbray, 1972.

Toynbee, A., *et al, Man's Concern with Death*, Hodder & Stoughton, 1968.

Trimmer, E., *Rejuvenation*, Robert Hale, 1967.

Wilkinson, J., *The Conquest of Cancer*, Hart-Davis MacGibbon, 1973.

Wilmers, M-K., 'A Very Nice Place', *New Society*, 12 December, 1974.

World Health, World Health Organization, April 1973, January 1974.